...just a girl with a pen

Due to the dynamic nature of the Internet, any Web addresses or links contained in this book may have changed since the publication and may no longer be valid. The author is not held responsible for the content contained in said web addresses.

ISBN: 978-1-257-06228-7
Content ID 10289739

Due to the nature of this book, some names have been changed to protect the identity of individuals mentioned. Some situations would be dangerous if their true names were given.

In Memory Of
Jeanette I. Hankins

This book has many thanks to be given. First must go to my Lord and Savior, Jesus Christ. There would be NO story if it weren't for Him.

Second of all I would like to say Thank You to my wonderful editor, Wendi Hansen. Without you, this story would have never left my computer.

I want to say to anyone that has had a dream, give it to God and chase Him. He will lead you on the right paths to reach the dreams He has for you. The course is sometimes bumpy, but it's always worth it! He will never leave you or forsake you. Thank you for embarking in this journey with me as you read what is to come in these next pages.

INTRODUCTION

I don't think I can qualify myself as a writer... really. I am just a girl with a pen that writes things down. I see, feel and experience things and I write them down. God has given me so many adventures and, I write those down. . . So, I don't think it is fair to think of myself as a writer. Instead, I will refer to myself in this story as a girl with a pen, writing down the things that have impacted me, changed me, and some of my mistakes, Most of all, I never want to forget the wonderful things that God has done.

You see, God is amazing, plain and simple. I could leave this at that, but I know there is a good reason why I am sitting down and putting these thoughts here on paper. I know that already, the writing of this will be done in a most interesting way...the way all things have happened in my life. Sometimes this has occurred beyond my understanding and I find myself wondering… Did that really just happen? Then I look back, and sure enough, it did. I am sure this story will be written in the same way, that when I look back, I will have that same sort of feeling.

I used to feel so small. I used to wonder what difference could I possibly make? What small thing could I even write that would make a difference? This of course is what Satan wanted me to think. Now I know that even my smallest offering, even in my weakest of moments, that God can and will use that to bring Him glory. In that, I know that I can make a difference in writing this story, even if the only difference is in me, I know that God is good, and I trust God to do His good thing…

There are so many ways that I could begin this. I know I will share my story, some of my friends' stories, Jesus' story, and a combination of all of it. I will tell you things that I have learned and things that have challenged me… oh so many things I can share! I will tell of all the crazy, wonderful marvels and even some things that may seem simple, things that God has completely surprised me in, so I begin.

For the first time in my life, the pages you hold in your hand are from my pen. I know that whenever I hold a brand new book in my hands the curiosity of what the pages ahead will hold takes hold of me.

I also feel it important to say that I, like Paul, the apostle was saying, am not perfect. If anything I am the complete opposite, I pray that you can hear my heart and know that I apply these verses to telling the story. Philippians 3:12-14 "I don't mean to say that I have already achieved these things or that I have already reached perfection! But I keep working toward that day when I will finally be all that Christ Jesus saved me for and wants me to be. No dear brothers and sisters, I am still not all I should be, but I am focusing all my energies on this one thing: forgetting the past and looking forward to what lies ahead, I strain to reach the end of the race and receive the prize for which God, though Christ Jesus is calling us up to heaven."

This story begins long before the foundations of earth, well before my body resides on, I won't go quite that far back in telling the story. My life is an adventure of being pursued by the love of my life, the King of all ages, the Savior of my soul, Jesus Christ.

I pray that you may you be inspired and hopefully see how wonderful God is, and that you may come to fall even more in love with him. Remember, I am nothing special, no author…just a girl with a pen…

CHAPTER 1

After a three hour trip in the back of a Sungtow (read: pickup trucks that have 2 benches on either side of the bed. Safe? Meh, I doubt it, but it is an extremely common way of travel in Thailand,) we had arrived to the place of the retreat we would be helping with. I knew that even in the Sungtow without being able to see, the ocean was parallel with the truck, and if I looked back over my right shoulder there would be an island. This was a rocky island that could look like a Hawaiian Island. Ahead to the right of me was another island a short distance from the shore. Just a little further down the road, if I were to look back, I would see that same island tucked away by two palm trees, and when the sun sets the island would shine like gold. I knew this place; at least my heart did. I didn't have to see it to know it was there. God had been preparing me for this moment.

You may be wondering, how did I know all of this? How could it feel like I had been to this place before? Well, you see, this was the place I had dreamed about for six months. I would wake up every morning with this picture on my heart; I could smell the ocean in my dream, I could feel the sun beating on my face and the gentle breeze in my hair. My heart would SCREAM for this place. Now, after months of prayer, a few closed doors, some wrong leads, and seeking and seeking God's heart on this, I was there. I was at the very place God had planned for me. Oh, He is so good and this isn't even the beginning, or the end, yet it is the place I must begin…

July 2008

Thirty two hours, swollen feet, three different flights and twelve time zones of travel were worth it all. Thailand. My swollen feet were now on the ground of the airport in Bangkok. Never in my wildest of dreams did I imagine that my feet would ever be in Thailand, yet somehow they were, on the complete opposite side of the world. I wish that I could say that I had been allowed to have some expectation of how the trip would truly look, but in preparing for this trip. God surprised me in more ways than one.

I was not allowed to prepare for the language, or really focus on the acts of this trip. I wasn't prevented by humans telling me not to, but every time that I would go to study, I would have the urging on my heart to go spend time reading my Bible and have some intimate times with the Lord. I had felt like I was being irresponsible when I was preparing to go on this trip, but it was close to impossible for me to study. Looking back on it, I think the Lord took any expectations that I had, and removed them all so I wouldn't put limitations on what God was going to be doing.

Stepping into Thailand was seriously like stepping into a different world, a different planet, but at the same time, one of the most amazing things ever. My first moments in Thailand were a little overwhelming. For one, my brain couldn't believe that this was an actual reality, and yet I knew that this was indeed real; and now that I had my feet on the ground my whole world would become a completely different place.

Even our welcome into Thailand was different than what we could have expected. We were welcomed into Thailand by a big sign that Randi, Kim and I were able to walk past without noticing. Randi and Kim are my long time friends that I was privileged to travel with. We have known each other for a long time and being able to travel with these women was a blessing I will never forget.

We had been looking for our friend Brandon, who used to live in the same place we did but now has relocated to serve as a missionary in Thailand. Instead of finding just Brandon, we also discovered several amazing Thai people were waiting for us. This was the most wonderful welcome I had ever experienced. We then packed ourselves, our luggage, and about 15 people into the back of a sungtow. This was a wonderful ride with the wind in our faces, all the while learning names, and the meanings of them in Thai. I have discovered I have an awesome skill of completely making a fool of myself and saying their names and any Thai word for that matter, completely horrible. I am grateful for their wonderful graciousness and kindness they showed toward me. I am grateful for the gift of laughter and kindness in mistakes with the language.

Seeing Brandon in the place his heart strings have been attached to was the most incredible thing. Here he is in a completely different culture, half way around the world, far away from his family, and he glows here. I love the way the Lord steals our hearts and places His love and faithfulness inside of us and leaves strings. He takes those heart strings and attaches them to places that He has worked in us and through us, and allowing us to grow more deeply in a passionate and intimate way with the Lord.

Somehow when I was in Thailand, I slept remarkably little, I would fall asleep later than the others and would wake up before them. I am not complaining; I had the most amazing times waking up fully with Jesus, and writing down everything going on in my brain. My first morning was no different. I woke up and something had changed in my heart. When I arrived in Thailand, I had been in the midst of a recovery of the heart and restoration of my soul. That morning there was just something that had lifted off of my heart being there.

If I thought the 32 hours of travel was a whirlwind, the first 32 hours of being in Thailand was even more. After the first night, I had already felt that I was at home, even though NOTHING resembled my life back in the States. There were a zillion cars on the road, taxis every color of the rainbow, no sidewalks for the most part, buses that had large open windows and writing I couldn't understand, dogs roaming the streets and it was HOT. Did I mention we hadn't gone more than six blocks from where we were staying? We were immersed in the Thai culture. We went to the most delicious place for our first Thai meal (which if I had a million dollars I'd pay to get some food from there right now. Sooo good!) We went to the Thai market and found fruit upon fruit were everywhere. Another great thing that was that I'd never have to cook while here! Every Thai food we could desire to eat was here at our fingertips.

Getting immersed into the culture, I am sure we had it easy, if I am honest. We met a lot of wonderful people that we became good friends with by the end of our trip, and our first church experience was an incredible place called New Song. This church was in Thai and English, so I can't say that culture shock was too extreme, but of course, none of this really matters. I go into detail so I don't forget, and so you can get a taste of the awesomeness of it all.

LORD where do I go from here? What are the words that you want me to write? I only want to write what you have me write, and so far I feel that this is not exactly the expression you would have me be writing in. Show me the words. Show me the way for my fingers to dance across these keys to form the rhythm that you would create. For you are all I am writing for.

Within 24 hours God was already doing things in our hearts. It's not like He ever stops or changes, just sometimes the things He is doing are more obvious than others. We went to the mall to check out a place Brandon was curious about, and ran into a Thai girl that spoke perfect English. She also had a friend that was an exchange student in Wisconsin. (My home state) Um, wait, what? Yea, that's right… welcome a new found friendship that we spent much time with for the rest of the trip.

It is amazing the way that God met us right away and with

such fervor. With our feet immersed in a new church, a new culture, and didn't miss a beat. The message at the church really began the pavement for the rest of the trip, and the things that God would be doing in not only my life, but in those encountered as well.

I was forced to examine and reevaluate the way God had made me, the way He had shaped me. The message relayed a pretty simple question, asking ourselves "Do we wear a mask?" From there "What kinds of mask do we wear, and do we truly display who I am in Christ? Do we quench him?" All of these questions and answers branched out in examining my life. We cannot fully serve the Lord if we are not honest with ourselves, and are being real because we are trying to be something other than what God has intended us to be. This doesn't mean not to try new things, or strive hard after something. It means being real and honest with who we are, and the things God made us to do.

There is a purpose for all things God created, all to give God the most glory. We give God the most glory in doing what we were created to do… and that is worshiping Him. Our lives can be a song, whether that is metaphoric or literal. Living that out brings God glory. I began thinking about what my song would be, and if I could only sing one song for all my life, what would my song be? I truly want to live with my life to be like the verse "However, I consider my life worth nothing to me, if only I may finish the race and complete the task the Lord Jesus has given me-the task of testifying to the gospel of God's grace." (Acts 20:24) I want this to be the resemblance of my life- being worth nothing to me, a vapor in the wind, a moment in time, only for the glory of God. God was beginning to remind me of who He made me, and what my "shape" is (Spiritual Gifts, Heart, Abilities, Personality, and Experience).

In writing this, I often find myself with a smile on my face, in remembering it all; trying to put into words all of the smells, feelings, sights, and the tastes. I can truly say that our trip was a series of divine interventions. Our team leader and friend Brett was did not arrive until our third day in Thailand. Because of this we still had some time before our team was assembled, and did a lot of exploring the area.

With Brett's arrival, our team had a day where we went to the Kings Park in Bangkok. This park was extremely beautiful, and the pond in the middle was even equipped with paddle boats in the shapes of swans and ducks. At the park, we prayed for the time we would be in Thailand, and the outreaches that would take place.

Pi Noy

One of our first interactions with the Thai was a facinating woman named Pi Noy. In Thailand you address your elders as Pi (Pea). We called her Yai Noy, meaning Grandma. She was a fantastic woman, and immediately stole my heart. Yai Noy lived in a pretty bad place on the outside of Bangkok. I assure you that on the way there, the roads were broken, and the cement ditches were filled with steam and sewer gases. We were on our way to the slums and it hadn't even gotten bad yet. We walked into this place that was a village, but it had more resemblance to a garbage dump for discarded things.

Their houses, if you can call them that, were on stilts that were sunk into the muck of green fungus, dirty water, and garbage that had been discarded. Their walls were decayed and the walkway between their houses was not even big enough for two adults to walk side by side. You could smell the water these shacks sat in. These are the people's homes, the place they slept, lived and ate. Their dwelling places were boards that were falling apart, and posters found on the side of the road, put together with tacks and rusty nails. If there was a toilet in the house, it was a piece of cement with a toilet, or squatty potty in it, surrounded by the swamp like water.

Yai Noy's floor in her house had fallen into the swampy grossness below. Her belongings, frail and old and what most people had already discarded, and then discarded again, hung in the mist of it all. The plywood floor had just given way and couldn't stay together any longer. When our team went to visit her, a different missionary team had been able to come in and was able to raise a floor to a room that would now be her entire living area. There was no kitchen, just a small room that had plywood floors and what looked like a table cloth for flooring to prevent slivers in your feet (in Thailand, you don't wear shoes inside). This room, to give you an idea of the tiny size it was, with her twin sized mattress inches above the ground, was entirely filled when six of us crowded around on the floor. It was about 7 feet wide, and maybe 15, barely 15 feet long. That's it.

This lady had immediately stolen my heart. I was instantly taken with her sassiness. It wasn't a real sassiness, but one I could get along with. It was a genuine love and gratitude. I wished to do something for her. I wanted to get up and redo her other room, the one that was dangling into the muck below, and yet, she would rather spend time sitting with us just keeping her company.

Writing this now makes me miss her very much, but again, she is twelve times zones apart, she probably has just got up for the day, and I am working on going to bed. She wasn't embarrassed by the shape of her house, or the lack of things she possessed. In fact her favorite thing she has was a picture of one of our team members that had visited before, and a picture of her deceased husband. Granted, for living in the slums, she did have her collection of things that probably should be discarded, but couldn't part with. Ah, yes, we are all humans with our tendency to hold on to some things . . .

I'll get back to Yai Noy later in this story but for now I'll move on. . .

The Slums

I believe the first day in the slums really was a breakthrough point for our team. The realization of where we were and the circumstances that our fellow humans live in were right in front of our eyes. It was no longer something we just read about, or saw on TV. This was now also our reality. It wasn't that we hadn't prepared ourselves the best we could, or had anticipated the concept of what exactly a "slum" would look like. It went beyond what we had dreamed of, seeing people going about their lives here, and for the most part, seemingly to be content.

Seeing Jesus, here in the slums, was definitely the most exciting thing. Here several of the people have come out of a religion that kept them in fear and shame. Seeing what the loving, living God of the world had done in this community was really incredible. While we were there in that swamp, we were greeted with hospitality divine; we were invited in to sit with them. It was almost unheard of to leave without having a snack and a soda or glass of water with them. While I realize that some of this is the way of the Thai culture it was taken to the next level. I see how Jesus had truly touched their lives, in a way that was so drastic that they wanted to live it, and extend that same grace, love, and mercy to the lives of all those around them. They truly had nothing, but they wanted to share all their belongings, and make you feel comfortable in their homes. They wanted you to come to their homes, even though you may not all fit inside. Sure, this may have been because we were farang (foreigners) to an extent, but I also saw how they treated the people from their own communities. It was such a blessing beyond words to be part of such a community.

A Literal Dream Come True

Our first major outing event was going to a retreat center along the ocean in Pattaya. This is where the story really unfolds. I will do my best to recap every moment, including my mistakes, and the way that God turns them around to have Him be glorified!

As we were riding in the back of the sungtow, the trip to Pattaya itself was amazing. There was something about the atmosphere of Thailand that just took my breath away. Some people say it is the humidity, but I think it was more so the manifest presence of God with us on these moments. We took several sungtows with our group piled in the back of them, getting to know each other and just sharing life with them.

As we entered Pattaya, my heart skipped a beat and my breath got caught in my throat. I knew this place. Impossible. I mean, I had never been to Thailand before those 36 hours had come to pass but yet, I knew it. It wasn't something I could know on my own, but it was a gift from the very creator of the world.

For several months earlier that year, I would dream about this place. The dreams were so specific; the fragrance, the temperature, the humidity and the exact location. I couldn't remember much else of what was to happen once I got there, but God had been clear in directing me, even though sometimes it felt like a massive wild goose chase, denying it for months and being told it was from demons and sorcery(I promise you I am NOT), I went to the Lord and asked, begged Him to take these away if they were not of Him, and help sort through what on earth these dreams meant. I was certainly NOT going to go chase a dream I have in my sleep with nothing to confirm it while I am awake. I mean goodness, I have had some strange dreams, but this dream was so very different. I couldn't shake it. It screamed! It made my heart feel like it was burning and crying for this place.

In searching for this place, God brought me close to His heart, and showed me I wasn't to chase this dream, but to chase Him and His heart; He would lead the way. So as I prayed, He would lead me in another direction, all the while I was reading His word and unceasingly praying. I'll get back to this again later but for now, I must go on… just don't doubt this yet…

Again, as we pulled in to town, and drove on by, my heart got excited, and was filled with peace, excitement, and anticipation. I knew I had found the place, and I hadn't even known how to look for it. I just knew that God would lead me to it when the timing was right….

CHAPTER 2

As I sat beside the ocean, with the breeze on my face, the fragrance of the salty water surrounding me, engulfing me with humidity much like a hug of a good friend, I looked out to the sea. Here I was, at a place that my heart screamed for, that I hadn't known how to find it, I didn't even know how to LOOK for it. . . I just knew that God would lead me to it, when the time was right; I just had to search and seek out God's heart. Jeremiah 29:14 tells us that God will be found by us.

Vividly, even now an entire lifetime or year later, I can still taste the air around me. I know the aroma, and I certainly can feel the air, the precise atmosphere surrounding me. More so than the location, I remember what God did right there on that beach, right where He showed, and lead me. I didn't even know what I was there for! Maybe it is hard to relate to this, because maybe you haven't had a similar experience, or maybe you have, but it was negative. I ask you to bear with me while I write and try to explain the majesty of what God did here in my heart and how I got to witness His truth being lived out. . .

The sun glistened over the rocky island, and danced across the ocean. I love the way God made the ocean to reflect and twinkle with the light of the sun, or moon for that matter, to shine across the expanse. I wish I could take you there, to see this. Instead, I try to paint a word picture so you can get a taste of what it looked like as well. The sand was crisp, laced with shells across the shoreline. The water danced along softly, coming gently over the beach. Ignore the televisions or other random "stuffs" floating in the water.

To the left as you stare across the vast blue sea was another shore line with buildings that looked like they were from a HUGE city; it resembled something that should belong on Jetsons' that old cartoon about the future. If we continue to turn to the left, we can see where the beach is filled with cots and umbrellas for tourists to come and relax and enjoy a moment on the beach. The street is protected from sight by tall palm trees, a color so vibrant a green it seems impossible to have such a rich color. The ocean itself was filled with Jellyfish.

Jellyfish

While I was in Thailand, I had such a difficult time gaining the confidence to speak the language, or try the language. After an epic failed try at the word "Thank you" (Kop Cuhn kah for me being a lady) came out sounding more like "capitan" or "capuchin", I struggled. The first Thai word I managed to master, remember, and actually was able to pronounce fairly well, was the word for "Jellyfish" (Man Ca ploun).

These creatures were everywhere. They consumed the waters of the Bay of Thailand. It was such an interesting time avoiding them in the water, but it still didn't defer some from embracing the awesomeness the water could hold. In some places it was very dangerous to enter, but the sweet bliss of swimming in that salty sea outweighed the danger. Sometimes you will get stung, but the experience remains. I am reminded of this as I think of my friend Steve who wasn't scared of the dangers that were in the ocean. Despite his courage he still ended up stepping on a jellyfish which had caused some pretty sweet damage. Now when I say sweet; we all know it wasn't truly sweet, it was painful, but still did not prevent him from entering the water in the first place.

What I am getting at is sometimes our life following after God is like swimming in a sea of jellyfish. There will always be some dangerous aspects that we may not see, but we can trust God. There may be some things that sting us along the way, but the embrace of the ocean around us is amazing just be able to be part of it. The jellyfish in the ocean remind me of the obstacles, dangers, fears, and demons that we have to face in this life. The ocean cannot represent God because there is no flaw in God, there is no evil in Him, but in following after Him, we will encounter painful times, we will encounter dangers. Our reaction to them, knowing when to follow Jesus at whatever the cost is always worth it.

There is no perfect image of God, because I don't think we can comprehend perfection. We know that God is the very essence of perfection and even the sound of that makes my mind boggle in the most amazingly wonderful ways.

God help me with these words. I am stuck with feeling like I am unworthy of writing, yet I know you have called me to do this. You put the idea in my head, and you give my fingers the rhythm you want to sweep across this keyboard and onto the page. God, I pray that your words will come out of my fingers and show them exactly where you want them to go. What are the words and what are the feelings and emotions Lord you want me

to share to show our relationship and your faithfulness? God, would you use my unworthy self to write this? Please make me strong in you, but not in a prideful way? Oh Lord, secure me in you.

A Song

Now, I need to back up a little bit and tell you about a friendly face I saw when I first got to the place we would be spending the majority of our nights. It was right after we had got off the plane and arrived to our destination; I was restless and excited. I could not sit inside. I wanted to be outside, even if we weren't in the best area of town, it wasn't the worst. I had to be outside. I stayed in the doorway of the building and the first person I encountered was this puffy blonde haired guy. Without knowing why, I knew this wouldn't be the last encounter with this person.

When we were in Pattaya for the retreat, I really felt strongly like I needed to go and find out this person's story and passion for life. I began to feel like a creepy stalker. God gave me a chance to find out why I first had this awkward inclination of why I had to get to know him. Please don't jump to conclusions; it wasn't in a romantic sort of way, but just in a sense that meeting him was significant in what God wanted me to do in Thailand. I don't know how else to better describe it, but I am sure Steve would tell you it was completely platonic.

I heard a voice singing; the most wonderful sound was coming from the chapel area of the retreat center we were staying at. I heard it and then I followed it until my ears could find where it was coming from. Inside was the blonde haired man pouring his heart out to the Lord. My friend and I went inside the chapel where I had attempted to go unnoticed, but more common than not, these sorts of things do not work out in my favor. This guy had the music living in him, straight from the creator, he sang with a passion and a love for God and it radiated out of him.

After chatting with him, I asked if he would share some of the songs that he had written, and I was blown away. While he was singing, and playing that guitar, I heard that still small voice saying I was to provide the means so he could have a guitar. When he was done singing, we talked about instruments, and he confided that he didn't actually own a guitar. Wait… what? I didn't dig out my money right then and there; I wanted to make sure after all the awkwardness of following him around, that it was actually the Lord and not me deciding that he needed a guitar.

The Beach

Somehow, I managed to go walking with my Thai friend Tukta and my friend Brett. I desperately wanted to see the image that the Lord had put on my heart for so long with all of those dreams. I couldn't just be in that location and not SEE it right? We went walking along the shore line, and it was the most breathtaking view I have ever seen. Here I was at that exact location. I stood soaking it all in, the fragrance, the sights, the sounds the gentle breeze from the ocean cooling over my face. I think the fact that I had seen this exact spot in a dream first made the experience all the richer. I could not have felt more blessed to have that confirmation of following His voice. It was everything I could try to describe to you, yet a bit scary, because I still wasn't sure why I was there. All I knew I was right where I was supposed to be.

While the sun settled below the horizon we took some pictures that turned out quite well but I still couldn't quite capture the view that was in my dream. I believe it will forever be etched on my heart and engraved in my mind. I look at the picture I took and my camera just couldn't capture the golden sun beaming and shooting light all around it. It didn't get the cascading clouds reflecting the awe. I still can't get the feeling out of my heart. I talk about it, and it's like I'm giddy with glee all inside; just amazed at it. It wasn't because it was so entirely perfect in beauty, but it was because it was a showing from God. It was the exact destination He had asked me to go. He doesn't always send us overseas to foreign beautiful places. I will get to that later in this story but when He does send you somewhere specific, He is going to get glory if we obey him.

Fear of Man

After we had taken our walk, it was simply beautiful outside. We called the rest of the group and suggested worship on the beach. I was so excited! First of all, worship is my favorite thing; second, I got to worship along the shores of the ocean. The ocean is entirely amazing, so vast, and it blows my mind away to think how big the ocean is and how much more the Father in heaven loves me, this tiny little human.

During the time spent on the beach, I really felt the urge to be a little separated from the group. I love being part of something corporate and of community, so I wasn't too far away, just a little bit down the beach so I could not be so easily distracted. I had my journal out with me, and I was singing and praising God and asking Him what He would have of me while I was there on the shores of the Bay of Thailand. I suddenly felt overwhelmed by the Holy Spirit, and never so much before had a peace settled on me, and His voice direct me clearly. I always get a little fearful when I write things like this, because for someone who doesn't know what I am talking about, they may think of me as crazy, but I tell you sure as day, God still talks to His children, He wants relationship, and He will go to whatever lengths He wants to get his word across.

As I was writing in my journal, I wrote how I had felt weird and slightly empty there that day; it was like my body had detached itself from my feelings. I am thinking it could have been jet lag even, but I had asked the Lord to turn it to peace and not be detached from my feelings. The Lord responded to me, and I didn't realize it at that time, but I pulled out my Bible that I had been carrying everywhere and began to read.

Journal Entry: July 15, 2008

-I love you God- Today has been amazing! I am enjoying today so much! God is blessing me beyond measure!
--Vision--
->May you NEVER tire of doing what is good. May you keep on pursuing righteousness and favor in the Lord, For He ALONE will supply all you need and all you desire will be made to HIS desires, all your desires, all your hopes swept away to be replaced with things beyond your greatest comprehension! What He takes away He will not leave a void. HE ALONE will fill it.

Like the waves, they come and go and have might, but none compare to the GREATNESS of the Lord! He will wash away, but give you a fullness of joy hope and LOVE! You may think you have holes in your life, but God will sweep over it like the waves, and fill all those spots with Him.---

Today as I mentioned, was beyond measure. If everyone could see what it is like to have faith as a small child...to be simply in awe of the Lord, if they could see a Thai love the Lord. . .

My heart is heavy for the institutionalized church, and how safe we have made God... when he doesn't promise safety... he does promise security. The safety he offers us is His safe keeping, but many people have been asked to step out into danger, to step into the face of the unknown, that is what the Bible shows and is full of.

I am so blessed this very second of my mere existence. I am sitting here on the beach, watching the waves crash over the shore, and think of Psalms 42:7 (NLT) " I hear the tumult of the raging seas as your waves and surging tides sweep over me." Now I know that David was talking about his deep discouragement, but the way that the waves crash onto the shore and how much God really does consume us like the waves crashing on the shores, how overwhelming it truly can be... overwhelming in a blissful way, or overwhelming in a heavy way.

*I look to my right, and see the island, the one of my dream, to my left and in the sky is the moon, mostly full. God spoils me so much, gives me so much joy and hope. ***

The Response

So, as I was sitting there writing the journal entry that you just read, God was speaking heavily to my heart. At that very moment I began writing, I saw that puffy hair blonde guy, and God told me to go put my hands on either side of his shoulders and pray for him. To this day, I can't help but wonder what would have happened if I wouldn't have negotiated with. However, I have to tell you as it did happen. As embarrassing as it is to know I disobeyed out of fear, I did it and God received glory from it all anyway. This is not my permission slip to disobey, because God asks obedience from us, but showing you that God will fulfill His purpose.

So here was that voice telling me to go pray for my spiritual brother Steve, and I almost got right up and did that very thing. Immediately, the warnings of the others that I was there on the trip with came to my head. These warnings had been addressed before we had even set foot on the plane to watch gender boundaries very carefully. I hesitated, and again, I heard "Go pray for your brother Steve, put your hands right there and there and pray for him." I begin to question what I was going to say. I am a girl; there are cultural boundaries, it is culturally unacceptable." The response I received was "Hey, Diana, I make the cultures. Are you going to pray for your brother Steve?"

At this point in my conversation with God, someone in the group suggested we go and pray for someone, it was like they could hear the conversation going on inside my mind with God. Only my female friend came over to pray with me. I told her we needed to pray for Steve, and she asked me what my motives where. I know she was looking out for me, but my motives were pure. So then I tried to pray from where I was at, all the while the anticipation in my heart was growing stronger. I had that urging that I can't deny in my heart, that I KNOW what I am supposed to go and do. Then the verse 1 Corinthians 1:27, "But God chose the foolish things of the world to shame the wise; God chose the weak things of the world to shame the strong" came to my mind and I heard that gently prodding just one more time, "Diana, are you going to pray for Steve?"

I didn't answer yes or no. I hesitated again, and I watched God do that very thing the verse says as he sent someone else to go do what I was supposed to do. As I was about to get up and do as I had been asked, I watched as someone else got to receive my blessing for obedience and able to pray for my friend, placing his hands exactly where God had told me to put mine. God showed me that His plan can be achieved, without me, that it is a blessing to be chosen to be used by him, and even a bigger blessing when we do as we are asked to do. It seems so often when we hear that voice, we want even more assurance, when God is waiting on us to do our part as well. UGH.

CHAPTER 3

Watching someone else do what I was directly asked to do was the biggest UMPH in my life. I failed at a blessing God wanted me to take part in, and watched how His purpose was still fulfilled. My brother still was prayed for, just without my help. Thankfully God did not leave it as that. While waiting to see if I got a second chance to make right what I had not done, life kept moving. He sent me on another short journey in the middle of all this; it was again nothing like I anticipated having to do. Sometimes we don't have a lot of time to make a choice; we have to know what is right and wrong . . . and repent and try to obey next time if we miss.

Vacant Eyes

A bunch of us Americans went to the walking street of Pattaya, but not for the common purpose of why people often go to there. The Walking Street is known as the red light district which is heavy in prostitution. I had known my expectations wouldn't be adequate for what I could prepare for. Going to a place where these women that are currently involved in prostitution would be unlike anything I had ever done. We had gone basically to pray for the people that were spread all around us, and also to open our eyes and maybe see if God wanted to share something that we could do, or prepare us for the future.

While we were walking through these streets, I witnessed so many people all in one place. My expectations were close to true, but what I hadn't expected was the feelings of all the women on the sides of the road. Let me try to paint you a picture of what it was like. Imagine a road of people packed moving in both directions, lights galore, a big spectacle, music is coming from all over, various fragrances tickle your nose and the biggest HEAVY, sad feeling ever. Even with all the media, the lights and entertainment, there was a heavy sadness. As we walked by these women, some who have chosen this career, and some that have the career choose them, looking into their eyes, watching their faces. I have never seen more desperation, emptiness, hollowness and hopeless expressions than ever before.

It is kind of surreal trying to describe it, because I don't feel I can adequately describe the scene in one paragraph; I don't have the words to describe it. Even in the midst of all of this hardship, the thing that rang true for me was "there is HOPE". I desperately wanted to go take these women by the hands and run them far away from this trap that they were in . . . However at that point in time I knew that my job was to pray and seek God for what my part would and could be. Hopefully, my writing this will make some impact that will last eternally. I desperately pray for those women and men seeking the women, whose hearts are far away, buried beneath the sorrows life has thrown at them, the things they have endured and the circumstances that have lead them to a place where their eyes are vacant when you look at them. Where they have lost hope, I have seen a way, and I know that God that loves these hurting people. If someone would just reach out. . . is it me? Is it you?

I know a lot that I have written about so far has been about the remarkably drastic things that I saw God move in. Yet I know he was there with me that very day I was on the walking streets, I know he was there with those very people with the vacant eyes, and I have to trust and believe that God is still moving in those very hearts. After all, as the band U2 says, "Sometimes change of heart comes slowly."

A Second Chance

Reflecting on my time on the beach I knew that God was teaching me obedience, and not just obedience, but hearing and trusting His voice. I knew it was Him urging me there on that beach, but I was scared of all the people around me. What would they think if I went to go pray for this man I hardly knew, why would I go and pray for him… and what would they think my motives were? It was already very clear that my friend questioned my motives, why wouldn't anyone else? God showed me that it did not matter what it looked like, it mattered what it WAS, my brother having a need to be prayed for, and God asking me to do it. If God says to do something, you better do it. Not because of the punishment you may receive, but because of the blessing you will miss out on.

The entire rest of that evening, feeling like a dog with my tail tucked between my knees, I had been praying that God would give me a second chance to see what I had missed out on. I repented, and asked Him to forgive me for my fear and inactivity as I completely feared what the people would say. After all, it was only my third day in Thailand, and I most certainly did not want to start things out on a bad note. Despite all my fears, and my inaction, I still could not help but wonder if the Lord would give me a second chance to find out what I was to pray for this person and what the results would be. I prayed that Steve would be awake when we got back so I might have a second chance to act upon God's urging.

As my team came back from the outing we had gone on, we stopped at the local 7-11 and my prayer had been answered. There was Steve, fully awake and going to walk back with our group to the retreat center we were staying at. Awesome.

Now I would like to say that I just went up to him and started chatting it up to find out what exactly it was that I was supposed to pray for him. That I would talk to him and get the depth of the conversation gong and find out who this guy was…but of course, I did not. I looked back and even laugh at myself with this, because the whole night I had been asking God for an opportunity to talk to this dude, to find out his story, to find out the mystery of the urgency in my heart to pray for him, and yet, I did not. Still trying to be somewhat sensitive to the gender differences and cultural sensitivities I looked around and I saw three girls sitting at a table so I walked up to them and tried to start a conversation…in Thai.

I knew enough Thai to start the conversation, and they knew enough English to keep it going, but then I had a sneezing fit and had to go find a Kleenex. I came back to discover my chair had been filled and I was no longer part of that conversation. Ok… I looked around, even though Steve was at the other end of the table, it would be pretty easy to strike up a conversation. I could hear in my head my other friend's warning about my motives, even though my motives were simply to PRAY FOR STEVE… I looked around and tried to find ANYONE else to talk to besides Steve. Real brave, right? Ha.

I won't say names because I am sure this person may be embarrassed that this in fact did happen, but I wanted to have a real conversation with someone. I really wanted to see who they were and what made them tick. I started a real basic conversation and asked a simple question to this person. Instead of a real answer, he pulled up his shirt over his ears and started walking hunched back, saying something about being Moses? At this point, I realized things were just going to become more and more bizarre unless I went to talk to Steve. This was the prime moment, because directly across the table from Steve was the only chair left. The only person not involved in a conversation…Steve.

Obedience

There I was, sitting across the table from Steve, I didn't want to freak this guy out, and making him think I was trying to hit on him or something ridiculous like that. I just really felt like God wanted me to pray for him and get to know his story. I asked God what I should talk to him about. I opened my mouth and began asking small questions, and pretty soon he was sharing his story. I won't share it in this part of the story entirely, but know that this man has a huge passion for the Lord that I hope never gets shaken, and that he never loses sight of this dream that God has instilled in his very being. It is a really encouraging one, and I know that God would use him mightily to do it.

As the conversation progressed, we got to the topic of the beach. As we were talking, I told him I hadn't obeyed God. I also told him while we were on the beach; I felt very strongly that I needed to pray for him. We continued talking for a while, and he shared that he too felt it weird, but that I was supposed to pray for him on the beach, but I didn't come. He said he thought maybe he had misunderstood, so he waited again, and still I didn't come to pray for him. He knew he needed prayer, so then someone else came to pray. Both parties involved had heard specific confirmations and both direction from God. Amazing. Too bad I didn't follow through, right?

Before I let my fear get in the way one more time, or I guess to confirm how crazy I thought he must have been thinking of me, (because I am trying to be obedient, but not so spastic) I hand over a bunch of money. This was for the guitar I had been told earlier in the day that I would be providing the finances for. Steve looked at me and was very quiet. I tried to explain that I still owed him some money and that I had wanted to wait to go the ATM and get all the money I needed first in order to be able to do this. I told him that I knew I had to be faithful in obedience and do it before I chickened out again. He looked at me, and quietly said "All day long, I knew I was going to get money from you for the guitar, I just didn't know how I was supposed to ask you."

I did get to pray for my brother Steve, sitting there at that table,. I was able to do as I was supposed to do, and pray specifically for what I was supposed to, down on the beach. I know often times we are not given a second chance to do something we messed up in, but sometimes God allows us to see what we would have missed out on and to help us overcome our fear of man, and come right to the presence of serving him. Steve had been asking direction, and what to do about China. God's answer "Steve, you need a guitar." It wasn't that Steve didn't need to know about going to China, it was just more relevant to the present that he had a guitar. God worked the timing of this out perfectly in changing the focus of prayer.

In the pages to come I will share of times when I would pray for one thing, but it wasn't what God wanted to speak about at that moment. I'll be sharing times when I don't hear from God and His voice, but in other ways he speaks . . . all in the pages to follow. I still struggle with trying to negotiate with God, I know some cool people in the Bible that got to negotiate, but I think God's got a better plan than I do. ☺ Besides, who am I to question God? Who am I at all? I'm just a girl with a pen.

What do you want me to put in this space, I desperately want my fingers to feel the keys only in the way you have. God, to remember what you have done, to be able to share in a way that brings you the most glory, God O Lord, how do I share all that you have done? How do I share how good you are? How do I remember even when I have forgotten! Lord, My prayer, my plea, I need you. I need reality, I ask that you direct my fingers again, and continue throughout telling this story.

Sunrise

That night we stayed up really ridiculously late, but I have never been so at peace about a lack of sleep. I think it was like 2 or 3 am that I was awake, yet, at 5 am I heard my friend Lu stirring about the room. I was awake, and not annoyed, but excited, I felt wide awake, like I had been awaken just for this moment. I asked her where she was going, and she wanted to watch the sunrise. . . yes…

I went with Lu down to the sandy beach and enjoyed some solitude time there, and enjoyed some time chatting with her as well. I watched Lu soak in the beauty of the beach, soak in the experience, and just capture the essence of everything to put in the depth of her memory. I love that I was able to be part of this whole beautiful scene. I know she probably would find it slightly awkward that I was watching. I was really trying to just enjoy the beach and the ocean, but there was something so pure in the way she was soaking in the whole scene.

While Lu was walking the shoreline, a stray dog came along side of her. This kind of thing is not unheard of in Thailand, but most of the time people just ignore that they are even there. They are considered a nuisance and just to be avoided, but Lu gave this dog some of her food, and played with this stray animal. I hope that I can be like this…only with people. The ones that feel neglected, overlooked, and stray . . . because I know how it feels. Watching her play with this neglected animal, I watched it go from being a little timid, to building a little trust and enjoying itself, perhaps remembering what it is like to be free and loved. I think watching her with the dog was even more beautiful that morning than the sunrise, and only because God showed me more of him through it.

Hope

After witnessing the most breathtaking sunrise, it was time for our group to leave the most peaceful retreat place ever. As we packed up our sungtows and prepared to leave the beautiful Pattaya, we were able to stop at an amazing place. Here in the streets of Thailand, in the Red Light district, was a glimmer of hope. There was a center for women who had been in the prostitution business; it helped to teach and train them to do different trades. It didn't matter what had caused these women to be in the sex trade, but here it was, a place to be set free from a trade that can degrade the body, mind, and soul of a human. These women were trained in baking, cosmetology, and beading, as well as handmade greeting cards.

In this little "shop" you could see the same women in the eyes of those that had been on the street, however they had been changed. These women have received hope; they received a new start, something fresh and new to do. They are no longer stuck selling their bodies. They found hope, and at the same time, Jesus.

There are so many things that may seem impossible; we get stuck in our crisis and our everyday life and forget to see the eyes of those around us. There is so much that we can do, if we start small, dream big and ask God what He'd like us to do. These women in that shop are so grateful for someone coming out of their comfort zone, to go and meet them in the place where they were to offer them hope, a new life and a future all in Jesus. It is a challenge to go and meet with these women, and change doesn't always instantly occur, but when it does it is a wonderful miracle. It is such a challenge to be willing to go into the places that aren't respected, to go hunt down the wounded, the broken and the desperate.

Sometimes these people feel that they are stuck and don't know there is anything else that they can do. I want to be a rescue worker in all I do. I want to be used by God to go find the lonely, the hungry and desolate. Jesus offers hope, because HE is hope. I also know that I don't want to leave any people to be fed to the wolves; these are my brothers and sisters through Christ. How willing are we to go to the really dirty places, places our reputations may be challenged? If God were to ask or if He were to be requesting how far would we be able to lay down our comfort zone and walk into the unknown?

CHAPTER 4

I almost didn't go.

Looking back at the way everything actually happened and how I almost missed it still makes me catch my breath. None of the things I witnessed, saw, tasted, and experienced would have ever happened. I am not even sure how to capture the crazy process into words, but I will ask God to help me with the words so He can get the most glory, and that you can see that I am just a girl with a pen, a human for sure.

Lord, where should I begin this chapter? Cover my fear in going to those places in life, and the judgment I felt. Lord, it is about you and your glory, not mine. I want your words to dance out of my fingers or I don't want to write this book at all. Lord, please show me the words and make my fingers write the words. If that is how I hear you right now, then let me keep going.

College

I started my freshman year of college at the age of 24. My

first year of college was filled with adventures of climbing things and homework parties where we stayed up late at night, sitting in a room with a bunch of other people that really wanted to be around people and accomplish homework. It worked well for me, not so well for others. Some of my most productive nights were the nights that the others were around me. They were often my encouragement, whether they realized it or not. They could be distracted by almost anything, but their distractions were enough movement for me to be motivated and inspired. Life inspires me.

Writing this book alone has been a challenge. I think I would do better if I had my dear friends sitting nearby, joining in their activities once I was finished. However, tonight it nears midnight and not many people are still awake in the small town that I reside. There is still a chance I will have a visitor tonight, but even so, this book brings back a lot of memories; memories of what God did, the things I was scared of, the things that God totally blew me out of the water with, even the hurts that sometimes thinking about brings back a twinge of pain that God is still helping me work out the details. I'll touch on those later in the story, for now I leave it as this. I love that sometimes small chances of possibility still make realities, my visitor just got here. I am blessed.

The Moon

My freshman year was filled with walks; I walked everywhere. My favorite nights to walk were the nights of the full moon. Since the time I was a cabin leader at a camp, the full moon has always stood as a reminder of God's amazing grace to me. I am sure most of the people that pick this book up have heard this analogy, and I don't mean to take credit for someone else's idea if it is theirs, but the full moon reminds me of my walk with God. The purpose of the moon is to follow the sun; the purpose of a Christian is to follow the Son. We reflect God's light at various stages in our life as Christians. Sometimes we get it right, and we are like full moons, where all people see is the radiating glory of God reflecting off of us. Sometimes we get in the way and we eclipse it, or we stumble, but if we keep following the Son, he will direct our path.

Ah, yes, there is something so peaceful about nights like this for me. The moon is out there shining brightly, just reflecting away, following the sun. Something I have failed to notice is that following the moon, there is a star. I've seen it before and have thought of it like a freckle in the night and now I can't help but think of the example Paul gave in the Bible to follow him as he follows Jesus. It is just a pondering that I don't have much more to elaborate on, but it is the glimpse that I get and the thought of how that even works. I am not saying that it means if people are following us because they idol us that they are in turn following the Lord. However, if they see the way we live, and follow the Lord we can be leaders as well. Regardless of our title or place in society.

One night not so long ago reminded me of my nights in college. I was walking around town and just seeing things differently when there was light reflecting on these places, the way the night sky looks was all the different too. I can't help but notice; there is just so much majesty in the creation around me, even in the creation that man has made. Not all of it is beautiful, but there is a lot of beauty.

For instance, I was walking along the ridge of the top of the hill in my town. Overlooking it in the dark, you can see a rainbow of colors. Dancing all over town, there are colors everywhere. The local businesses and street lights were creating this vast glow, even though this is a small town.

Then near the courthouse, there was this stairway that leads down the steep hill. The destination isn't what is important here; it's the sweet imagery of it, the lights on the side of the railing!

Reflecting and leading the way for all of those that chose to follow. It is splendid. It is in the light that I see the small glimpses of hope everywhere.

His light will shine. He is the KING of the universe. We are the reflectors, but we reflect by letting him love us, change us, and work through us, allowing His intensely deep love ravishingly change our hearts.

Having A Voice

When I was in my early 20s, I lived in a town in Michigan. I could probably write an entire book on my Michigan experience and the marvelous things that God did in my life, showed and taught me. However, that time is not today. When I lived in that town, it was a place that God used to help me grow even more in my faith, showing me how it was mine and His and how to stand in it. The interactions that I had with the Lord there were intense; it was like I had a direct line telling my body which direction and which movement my body should make at every moment. I am not even sure how to fully describe it; it was just a Holy Spirit thing. I reflect highly on my Michigan experience because it is a milestone in my heart, and it was where God gave me a voice.

When I lived in Michigan, we were constantly meeting people; we were at the coffee houses, we were on the streets playing hack, in the parks, etc. We were just everywhere that people were and in doing so; we would talk to them, and invite them to hang out with us. In the process, we sometimes were able to share Jesus with these people. Not in a forceful, awkward way, but just in sharing what the Lord has done in our life. Because he has done things, amazing things, as cliché as it sounds, I was lost, and now I am found. I am saved from eternal damnation and I have salvation. One of the things we always did was sing. There is also something different between singing a song and worship, and I was learning about true worship, telling God what He is worth, and the one time we get to do something in return for God. I loved it.

Only catch. I couldn't sing. Not nicely, but I sang anyway. All the time, I asked God if He'd give me a voice if I'd use it for Him. First He taught me about Joyful worship. Ah, yes, Joyful worship, singing and making music to the king in joyful adoration. It doesn't matter the quality of the sound, but the heart condition. More and more I am learning that our human hearts hold a guard around itself. Sometimes a few songs are required to be sung to let ourselves let that guard down, and enough to be humbled and then enter into an amazing, intense, and intimate connection with the Lord through song. It is just an incredible way to pour ourselves out so He can pour back into us. It empties us when we give God everything in singing our praises, and prayers to the king. There is something so in depth about music that I know God made to help us connect with him even more.

Then He surprised me. He didn't have to grant my request, but He gave me a voice anyway. I can tell when it is Him singing through me because, if I can humbly say, and take myself out of the situation. WOW. He is good! He has totally blown me away with it. He has filled me with passion for Him and connecting that way. It doesn't always come out sounding fantastic, but when he sings through me, it always sounds better. I now hold a much better singing voice when I use it for Him.

For many years, God made me realize I had a voice. For all of you who know me, you know I have a voice. By saying this, I don't mean necessarily a beautiful singing voice, but I do have a voice; one to sing, and one to speak and stand against injustice and one to join in glorifying God. I speak my mind, God gave me this voice, and I will not stand silent when a voice needs to be heard. If that means a vocal voice or the voice of action, I want to use it.

I kind of have been feeling for a very long time that I am supposed to use my voice, use the things that are in my heart and shake the world with it. I love, love, love, love, the Lord Jesus. He is so wonderful beyond words. I am so romanced by HIM! My heart sings. There used to always be a song in my heart, a song on my lips, always. Then, there was a time that was kind of silenced. Not on purpose, but more so there was a struggle. Not with my faith in God, but my relationship with Him wasn't where it should have been. I relied on Him for survival instead of having the relationship that I so craved. I was physically and mentally drained. I was deceived and struggled with physical pain that caused a great deal of stress and my voice kind of faded in the process. Anyway, at some point, I wasn't singing all the time. I still had Jesus in my heart, but I wasn't feeling His entire joy. I am aware that we can't always rely on our feelings, but joy sometimes is one that is so much easier when it seems tangible. Somewhere in there, the song had become silenced. I find myself facing this same thing even now when I feel really defeated by either my health or other disappointments and rejections that it's hard to hold the joy when everything is trying to silence it.

Without realizing it, I've pushed aside a passion that I always thought was something between me and God. Where I still sang and did music for him but I wasn't doing it as often. I had moved locations and the opportunities weren't really available for me. I didn't have the same skill level as the others that were invited and asked to share their music. It hurt a great deal at first to go from being able to have places to use my voice to a place where there were not the opportunities. After a while, I kind of gave up trying to find a place to sing, after a while I kind of just forgot. If you don't use something, you lose it. It pains me to know the practice I had and the improvements that I could aid with have since faded. I know God can revive this passion if there is someplace to use it.

When I lived in Michigan, I had a once in a lifetime opportunity to sing with a band called Fusebox. I never had the desire to do so before, but randomly while at a conference, I had a strong urge to go to talk to the lead singer. I just randomly asked if I could sing with them. He said yes. My mouth dropped with shock. Number one, shock of what I just asked and two, he said yes. I then asked two of my friends to join me for this honor. I knew when I was on stage that God had something in mind for me; to use my voice, whether it is by singing and leading people in worship, teaching people about worship, or just speaking, or in this case writing.

I have a voice. How God wants me to use it, I still don't know entirely how that looks. Part of it may be writing this story. It seems every time I try to use my vocal singing voice, I get turned down. I know I need to rely so heavily on Him, that He is the one that puts the song in my heart and on my lips. He is my savior, my best friend, the center of my life. I love my Jesus. Life is so full and real with Him. He is alive.

Without going into too much more detail, when I moved from Michigan, I was completely unprepared for the difference in the way that God would talk to me. I know there will be another entire book coming after this one to include those experiences. Sigh, I have a lot of finger dancing on these keys to look forward to, but at the same time, wow, all the more for God to get glory. Anyway, I didn't dream dreams that I knew were from the Lord, I didn't have that direct "go here" instinct, or felt like I had; God was teaching me in a different way. His word always trumps all; I always go to His word and have Him confirm things while I am awake. In a span of a few years, a town, and a car accident in the middle, I was used to not hearing from God in that way. I still believed in Him but only heard him in the peace of my heart when I would pray and read His word.

The Return of A Dream

On New Year's Eve 2007, I was in the cities at a conference. Finally, I could FEEL the manifest presence of God. Now I know not everyone is able to feel these things; don't worry, it is ok! God has different and cool ways to speak to you; just be prepared and open your heart to Him. Not everyone is going to hear Him speak in the same way, but He is always talking to us. The most amazing thing is that we have this perfect book that is a letter to us, His people. We get to not only see how it impacts our lives now, but also the relationships that God had with his people then and how it looks for today! Wowza!

It was at this conference that I was talking to God. I was off to the side and was desperate for some solitude and not to be bumped into. I needed space so I wouldn't be distracted. I was singing again, getting into the music, and I heard a voice asking me how much I loved God. I said, "Oh forever" and I all of a sudden felt I had to go to my knees. I was not able to stand. I became so amazed by how unworthy I truly was, and how much God really, really, really loves me. Soon, my knees didn't seem to be the place that even felt like I was worthy to kneel on; I felt extremely silly sprawling myself out on the floor, but this was a moment with the Lord. I lied in the middle of this conference with thousands of people, sobbing and crying out to God. Again, details aren't important, but God allowed me to speak to him through my tears and He opened up that line of communication. Once again, I began to dream, little dreams, and I didn't even know that they were happening for a little while longer.

Hawaii

After my freshman year of college, I was able to go to Hawaii and visit my friend Ami and meet her husband Hugh with another one of my good friend Corissa. Besides being a really fun vacation, God began to speak louder to me. His creation was beautifully depicted in this lovely place; WOW! The first night I was there, I had a dream and the next day, it came true. I prayed the whole next day trying to figure out what the meaning of it all was. I still to this day am not sure the purpose of the first dream, besides giving me a confirmation of it, but I didn't remember until AFTER all the stuff had happened.

The next night, I again had a dream in color and I woke up with that HUH feeling, that the dream was significant. This is not true for everyone, but I have learned that most of the time, when I dream entirely in color, those are the ones that come true. The ones that have some color and some black and white are learning dreams and the ones all in black in white are "just for fun." Those are not always fun, but you get the general idea. Again, this is just what I am beginning to realize after much prayer and studying. This dream proved itself real 9 months later. I had a dream that my friend was pregnant, and going to have a baby girl, which she didn't want to believe. It wasn't my idea or thought; I couldn't have imagined that. However, I could see it in her eye that she wanted it to be true. I cannot say I understand why God allowed me to dream this. I just know that God gave this dream, and it was again the beginning of a whole new year.

CHAPTER 5

The sun was intensely hot, the air humid, but it didn't feel gross. The wind was subtle and gently touching my face as a delicate silk would fall gently over my skin. The soft crash of the waves joining with the shoreline sent a small cascade of droplets onto the seashell covered sand. The sun shone brightly and made the sky an amazing, brilliant gold as it reflected and danced across the ocean and hung behind the rocky island. The air smelled of sea salt, a slight hint of some sort of flower and lingering residues of a spicy food. A perfect peace settled in my heart, and I felt embraced.

"Boaaammm bump bump bah dah dah dah…" the theme song from Fraggle Rock stirred me from this place. I opened my eyes and it was like the depth of my heart demanded for this place that I had just come from. I don't know how to describe it; my heart screamed and there was an ache and almost an emptiness that the depth of me could not shake. Almost every day I would awake with this image etched in my heart. I could open my eyes and it would still be there, it never left, it was just there.

At first, I tried to brush it off and believe I had a great

vacation and was missing Hawaii. After all, my mind could easily have made this image of Hawaii, even though, I hadn't seen it before. I asked God every night what the dream meant and to help me shake Hawaii off of my mind. The dream continued. Not only did the dream continue, but it stirred so deeply in my being, the longing for this place I did not know grew. I ached and became heartsick.

I should mention, my life did not entirely wrap around this dream, but it lingered throughout the day. I was able to still live my life and focus on God and my school work, but it still never left my side. I decided not to tell too many people about this dream. For one, if I was crazy and being lustful for a place, I wanted to be sure I was sharing it with people that may pray for my understanding what it meant, if there was a meaning. I am a pretty open person; I believe in being real, open, honest and a little vulnerable, so I wanted to be able to share this with someone. By all means, at this time it had been at least 2 months of almost every morning waking with this image engraved on my heart.

After two months of this, I remember pleading with God to either take this dream away or make it relevant and help me know what it was I was supposed to use it for. I don't know if I can even begin to try and describe the heartsick feeling I encountered every morning when I woke up. It was the most fierce, undeniable experience in my mind. I couldn't shake this. I was kind of getting annoyed, but at this point, after praying about it, and nothing happening, if anything the dream became more frequent, I decided and prayed that it was time to change my approach.

I started seeking more the heart of God. I started seeking in the scriptures, for who God is, and His character and His nature and just digging in and trying to get to know him more and more. If I wasn't going to understand the meaning of this dream that wouldn't leave me alone, I was going to know my Lord more and more.

I also started sharing little with some people I thought I could confide in. I encountered some people that were honest in seeking and helping me work through this with the Lord. There were those that shared their doubt with me, but still were honest. The worst I encountered were those that thought they knew it all, or pretended they didn't think they did… and passed judgment, condemning my dream. They immediately, upon me saying that I had a dream that I wasn't sure the meaning of but at the same time was trying to seek God out in it, freaked out and said I was into sorcery and witch craft. Unfortunately, I know these things happen. I also know that when God gives dreams and visions, there is always the chance that we can have dreams that are awful and not from God. Or ones that are tricky. However, I know that if I were to disqualify this because it was controversial or because people were mean, rude, and just plain hurtful about it, I would have missed out on seeing God's glory.

I remember crying out to God, asking if I really was following sorcery or witch craft unintentionally. Why is it that I am having dreams that are coming true and I don't know the entire meaning in it? I cried as I poured over scripture and asked Him to show His heart to me. I did NOT want to be pursuing something that couldn't be confirmed when I was awake, and I did not want to give credit to something that didn't deserve it. I just wanted Jesus in this. OH MY GOODNESS! I was so frustrated! I was just so desperate for wanting to seek out what God wanted me to do, without focusing too much on the dream aspect.

Lord, I know your truth needs no justification. Please direct the words and help me be able to display what you would like through my fingers. I know you have a good plan for this and I want to be able to seek what it is that you want me to do with it. Help me write this and how you confirmed things with me. I want to share all the things to be real so that you will be seen though the doubts, through the hurt, and how you turned it into something amazing.

A New Approach

At this time, some other action was due to take place. I couldn't keep these current happenings continuing in the way they had been. So, I prayed for a different thing and in seeking God's heart, I started trying to figure out what this meant. My new prayer had become something to the effect of, "God, I will follow you. I am going to need help finding this place. I will go to where it is, if you show me how to find it as I look for you". I remembered the image to resemble Hawaii, and I began praying for the direction if it were Hawaii, and if it wasn't where to go from there. So, I began praying and investigating opportunities that I would be able to go to Hawaii, and this time, for more than a ten day vacation. I knew that it was supposed to be longer than a week, and I knew it would look different.

In one of my classes at school, there was a representative that came from a study exchange program and something moved inside my heart. I didn't know if it was my own curiosity or if it was because I was now looking for something, but I kind of began leaving things more in his hands; I took a bookmark and set it aside. Several weeks later, I came across it randomly and found myself getting excited at the possibilities that could unfold.

This program that found me allowed a student to study in a different state for a semester. It was a lot like studying overseas, but without the need of a passport. I was pretty excited as I wandered around the website for more opportunity. The school I found was in Hawaii and had the current program that I was in for my major. Sweet! I set up a meeting with an advisor and continued praying with my Bible readings as well. In my interpretation of this, I should be right on track, easy peasy, right? I gave up fighting and I went; I was well on my way back to Hawaii . . . right . . . or not.

My heart was immediately let down when I found out that the school that I was looking at in Hawaii did not accept people unless someone from that school decided to come to my school. Ha ha ha.

That would mean people from Hawaii wanting to hang out in the frigid state of Wisconsin for winter? Right. . . Immediately, I began praying my doubts, "Ok, God, I am not mad. I am really trying to find this place. I am trying to obey you. I don't know what that looks like in this, I don't know what it looks like at all, but I want to go where you want me to go. I went and tried to follow you to the island and I thought it was Hawaii…" and continuing on. The advisor was talking but I wasn't doing a very good job of listening to her and then a folder for Fiji literally fell into my lap.

Great. I am going to Fiji… At least that is the next course in the track for which I thought God was leading me. I mean the folder FELL into my lap. However, this again was another stepping stone in the treasure hunt to chasing God's heart. When it fell in my lap, that still small voice in my head that I heard didn't make sense to the current things sitting on my lap. When I asked God about Fiji, the answer I heard was nothing to do with Fiji but was instead about "Brandon, Thailand".

At this point, I was still wondering what this meant. I was trying desperately not to read into things, or place my interpretation on it, because I had been wrong with Hawaii; I didn't want to be wrong with Fiji. I just wanted God to let me know what I was supposed to be doing! I hope you can hear my frustration in this treasure hunt, but I also hope you can hear how God was drawing me closer to His heart, drawing me closer to His plan and the things that He had for me, and not just me, the people that I would encounter.

When continuing to pray about Fiji, and what I was supposed to do, I continued to hear "Brandon Thailand." I should mention here that Brandon is a good friend. When I lived in Michigan, his family welcomed me in their arms, took me under their wings and treated me like I was another one of their children. Brandon is very much a brother and a friend and an amazing man of God. I knew kind of in the back of my mind that Brandon was in Thailand doing ministry of some sort and I had lost contact, for the most part, with this friend.

In praying for Fiji and continuing to hear "Brandon, Thailand" as the constant response that God gave me every time I prayed, I remembered that Brandon had gone to Fiji on an outreach at some time in his life. At least what I could have started to do was investigate what was up with Fiji; it couldn't hurt as far as I thought. I sent this friend an email just seeing what he had done while he was there, not asking a thing about Thailand or anything other than what he had done in Fiji several years ago.

Several weeks had gone by and I still had the dream, but the intensity had been lessened by the pursuit of God's heart and desires. When I stopped seeking God's heart and started focusing on the dream, the turmoil returned, so I continued directing my focus on God and what He had for me that day.

I was at work and I was allowed to have my computer on. While working on my homework, my instant messenger notified me that my friend Brett was on so we started chatting. At this point in time seeking God, I had kind of thought if an opportunity to go to Thailand presented itself, I would have to seriously consider going. Remember at this point, I hadn't told anyone that Thailand had ever come into my mind when praying for Fiji in this treasure hunt. We started talking about just random things and he brought up Thailand. (Brett is Brandon's younger brother.) Brett sent a message saying he was going to Thailand and then fairly sarcastically added, "You should come too" and then, "WAIT, YOU SHOULD COME!"I don't know if I can express the excitement and cartwheels that went on inside my soul. Peace. I finally had peace. I didn't know if this was going to be the location of the dream that I saw, but I knew that I was going to have to pursue this in pursuing God's heart.

I remember writing back to Brett with the response of, "Maybe" and that I would pray about it and get back to him. In my studies at school, readings in the bible, and times in Church, the messages where all about God's heart and being willing to be obedient. We talked about Abraham and his willingness to sacrifice Isaac; God provided the animal for sacrifice, and Abraham had to go and prepare and believe that he was following God. He was being obedient and forced to trust God. I am amazed at this crazy image. Think about it in terms of today. Who is willing to do something that seems so crazy like taking your son, the one that you were promised by God, go to the mountains, into the woods, and um, get ready to kill him. Wait, what? Who would do this now? Let's be real; we all want to say we will and be the hero of the story, but do we really believe it? I don't have a son, but I can't imagine being asked to take him and get ready to kill him, trusting that God was going to provide a way out.

I wish I could remember more the things God confirmed while I was awake so I could document it better here in this story. I was certainly not looking for signs to come to me or reading into things in seeking this place that I was dreaming about. I just wanted God and His heart. I know I freaked out most times and still go into freak out mode when trying to understand what God is saying. What I am learning more and more is that the destination isn't always what is important. Sometimes he will show us a destination so that we have something in our mind to look towards, spur us on and seek Him out. My focus shouldn't be on the gift, but the giver of the gift. He's going to be the one that made the gift, help me use it, and teach me how to use it in the right timing.

So now that going to Thailand was presented to me and we would be going to see Brandon, I began to think: this was the next step in following God, finding out what this dream really meant. I prayed about Fiji one more time and remember saying, "God, what about Fiji?" You know what answer God gave me: "Brandon, Thailand." (Does this sound familiar to earlier in the story about a guitar and China?)

Now how on earth was I going to GET to Thailand. . .

CHAPTER 6

Fear is a crippling thing. Tying doubt with the ever so famous "responsibility" can also be terrifying things that can get in the way of God's plan. I am not saying to be recklessly irresponsible, but it is far more important to follow the voice and follow God than trying to be responsible for something we were never asked to be responsible for. . .

I remember the feeling that was inside of me immediately following the instant messenger conversation with my friend Brett. It is inexpressible, but I will do my best to put into words where I feel that there are no words to describe it. There was an excited peace that swooped through the veins in my body. Not the kind of excitement you get because you are trying something new, or going on a fun vacation, but the peace that this is what you are to do, the peace of assurance, the excitement of that, and all the possibilities it holds.

The next several moments were surreal. I was still at the hotel working and yet I felt like my feet had left the ground and something really exciting was about to happen. Yes, I knew I was going to Thailand. I didn't have a clue how I was going to pay for it, but I knew my taxes would be coming back shortly and that maybe they would be enough to cover the trip. I just knew that it was my treasure hunt. The rest of the day at the hotel was a complete blur. I remember doing my job and not being able to wait to get back to the Holty's (my friends' house that I was staying at) to talk it over with them.

Prayer became my lifeline. Even more than before, I began to pray for this trip and how I was supposed to pull it off. What were the means that I was to trust God in providing for the funds to go? When was this trip supposed to happen? What was my involvement for preparation? Questions and thoughts flooded my mind. I now think it was a great thing that I had college classes to keep my mind somewhat occupied on other subjects because I felt like a child in anticipation for Christmas or their birthday, awaiting the surprises and magical feeling that they bring.

In preparing to commit to the trip, I prayed consistently; for direction for the trip, for God to reveal his heart to me in His word, and to teach me more about Him. My good friends, who I found trustworthy, were able to share with me in the excitement of praying and preparing for this trip of the unknown. I had no idea what it would look like, what we would fill our days with, or anything at all. It was our trip; we would plan it, and execute it.

Lord. Here I am again, at your feet, humbly wanting to write your words. Help me remember what you would like me to remember. Share how your glory worked through my doubts, my fears, and how you worked through them all, showing me closed doors, sometimes by painfully running my face into them and when you showed me quickly which step to take and which

direction to go. Lord, it is only you that is capable of writing this story. It is your story; I was just the mere body that was blessed to take place in it all. Let me embrace your splendor and the way that you did such amazing things and allowed me to be part of it all. Lord. Jesus, I do not ever want to tire of your beautiful name, your beautiful grace. I want to know you more and more. Help me seek your face even as I write all this down. Where would you like my fingers to go next? What would you like me to write?

The Jungle

In my second year of college, I lived in a house that was named the 'Jungle'. It was a house full of five females between two stories. The townhouse was equipped with two bathrooms, a living area, a kitchen, and enough bedrooms for each of us to live. It looked like the perfect place to live. However I think any of the roommates that lived there that year would disagree fiercely. Our personalities did not go well together; there was always a war of miscommunication and accusations between some of the roommates.

While most of us got along individually, there was always a tense awkwardness inside these four walls, so much so, that I did NOT want to spend any more time there than I had to. I felt completely incapable of being able to be myself; there were unwritten rules that were imposed on others and honestly, I can't describe the grossness of living in this place. It felt like a complete and literal jungle, lost in a mess of deep darkness. It hurt and felt like I was constantly running into things. We had tried to establish a working form of communication between the roommates, we had tried to maintain peace, but there was something about it that was just off.

There were some good memories I had their, like getting

dressed up and going to the park and swinging with one of them. I will keep her name a secret simply because I do not want anyone's name to be associated with this house. I have some really decent memories also, but overall the experience was less than amazing.

When I look back on it, I know that there is no way to describe the awkward, tense, almost defeated feeling that happened while living in those four walls. I know I called out for outside help quite often, in fact. I am sure one of my best friends, Jacob got more text messages and phone calls asking for prayer than I remember sending. All I know is, if I could accurately describe the warfare that happened, the literal attack against us living there, you may understand. I feel that no words will work, so I am not really sure why I am still typing, but just know that it was not pleasant and I wanted out.

Looking back, seeing it a year and a half later, I can see that it was in this struggle that made me cry out to Jesus more and more. I don't think I did a great job of looking to Him; I am sure that I failed many times. I just wanted him to send a rescue, to make the ridiculousness go away. I do know that on those days when I felt I couldn't pray myself or when I needed reinforcement, I knew to send out prayer requests for prayer warriors. I know it was the prayers of many that kept me going and that kept me safe.

The Eyes of Others

While living in those four walls, it was a jungle in my life, a wilderness, a journey. If living in those four walls wasn't enough to learn and grow from and be challenged, even though I felt like my very being was being ripped apart, there was more. There have been few times when I have felt that the eyes of others have been so heavy upon me and my life that I have no room to move, to breathe, to do anything. It was like they would wait for a crack, a moment of even greater weakness, and then they would strike.

This time though it came among the very people that I thought should be there, encouraging, helping me walk it out. Instead, I received judgment; no one wanted to find out why I was doing things the way I was doing them, no one wanted to find the source of my tender, broken heart. I was told to buck up, deal with it, and was given more advice that was not asked for by so many people that didn't know the story at all.

I don't share this information to make me look like a better person and them the enemy; that is not the case at all. In fact, I just beg you to open your eyes to what this says. Seeing this time and time again, I want desperately to make a change in the body of believers. I know that I have not always looked at what is the cause of someone's actions, regardless if I think they are right or wrong. I assure you that though I am not perfect, I cannot see any major sin that I was living in that would cause judgment. The only thing I saw was that people did not understand me, therefore deciding I was now to be "fixed" instead of understood.

Experiencing this has made me long to find the source of an action, to try and understand where someone is coming from. I certainly do not want to put a band aid on a broken bone or a cast on a beauty mark. I speak from negative experience hoping that I can be part of a positive change, and maybe someone that reads this story will also take heart. If I truly want to be a help in this world, I have to be slow to judge, quick to love, and quick to listen. I have to make myself available to listen and be a safe ear. This does not mean I grant you to live however you chose; there are specifics that the Bible says, but how can I expect someone to know something they haven't ever heard?

While dealing with this and trying to walk it out with God…meaning trying to figure out my part was, how much was

God's part, and how to live in surrender and try to overcome this fear.... I desperately wanted to be in the will of God, seeking what He wanted me to do, rather than what everyone else thought I should do. I am not lessening the credit to wise counsel, but ultimately we belong to Christ. He needs to be the first one we follow. First seek him, and continue to seek him.

Everyone will always have some sort of advice that they want to give and a solution to problems you didn't even know you "had." The best thing we can do is try to not focus on that attention we are getting. It can be really confusing hearing God's voice when we have a lot of people that know Him trying to tell us, when maybe He just wants to talk to us Himself. He gave us His word, His written word, and He has spoken a variety of ways to people over the ages. How does God want to talk to us? Have we laid down my ideas of how we want it to look? Do we have a mental picture of God? Does it only look the way He talked to generations of the past? I am not trying to persuade you to do something funky, but maybe ask yourself and look to our ancestors, how did God talk to them? Did that stop? God is all about relationship; sending His son Jesus shows us a fantastic picture of that. Wow, I can't even begin to think about it. I know we have heard the gospel time and time again, but wow!

Think about this: I don't care what age you are and I am sure some of you will skip over this part because you already have heard it; it has become common but if I can grasp your attention for another second. Take a breath and deeply think about this. Imagine if it were now, what would Jesus' death and resurrection look like? Imagine your very best friend, in human form. You see him, you feel him, and you can even smell his scent.

You know the sound of his voice because he is right in front of you, living, breathing, a tangible being! Something you can put your hands on. Your best friend stood up for what was right, never sinned, never did anything that was wrong and now he's been taken to prison, and not just the prison that takes you away from home, but this is one of shame, humiliation, and physical abuse. Now, you know that you have done wrong many times; you should be there in that prison, not him! Not this man. You can still talk to him, still hear his voice, still smell his scent . . .

Then, they kill him. Not just quietly, but the most public horrific event ever seen. Your best friend has taken the punishment for all of the people you see, some of those people you don't recognize, some you know very well. Still here he is, taking the punishment, and he's about to die. Oh my goodness, can you truly imagine this??? Right there in front of you; what would you do? Would you feel helpless to do something? Have you really put the face of your best friend there? Because it makes it more real to me… because I think sometimes we forget God was flesh and blood, He BECAME LIKE US! Um, what? Yeah. That's amazing. If we could fully grasp the life of Christ, the full meaning of grace and redemption, the power of his coming back to life, (less fancy way of saying resurrection) wow! I know we'd be living a lot differently…

Obstacles

I sometimes get confused with the difference between a closed door and an obstacle. I am still learning when I need to keep looking and when I need to stop. I don't think this is a lesson that can be learned over night and I am excited for the process, even though I know it may be painful, because running full speed into a closed door hurts. A lot. This journey and part of the story is no different than another.

Excitement mixed with fear is the most bizarre experience. There were so many fears that gripped me in thinking about this trip. I kept hearing the nagging voices that I may be in some weird sorcerer-witch craft kind of thing, and my brain kept wondering what the ones that accused me of such things would think if I was pursuing a dream here, a literal dream. I also have never in my life wanted to go to Thailand before this trip. I have my list of destinations that I would love to see and I am not sure why Thailand hadn't made the list. I think it was to bring God more glory in this story, because it obviously was not a "Diana desire," especially if I had never wanted to go before! The timing scared me too! How was I going to find a job that would let me work for them and take all this time off in the summer? That brings up another remarkable thing; how on earth was I going to find the amount of money for a plane ticket? What would our group do? What should our group do?

Somehow in my fear, I didn't experience worry, or at least worry that paralyzed me. I remember being curious, but oddly at peace. It was scary, but in a wondrous kind of way. The biggest thing that kept me wondering how God was going to have this trip happen was the plane ticket. This was a large chunk of money. I knew it wasn't out of the grasp of my God's hand, but still this could be a determining factor if I would be partaking in this adventure, or trying again to see what I was supposed to be doing. I remember talking to Brett about using my income tax refund, but when I received that, some unprepared for expenses came up, and it was gone sooner than I could even blink my eye. Confused and not certain of what would happen, I still felt like I was going to be going on this trip.

CHAPTER 7

On June 7, 2005 my life had taken a jolt. After a year of a different jungle and really ultimate difficult season in my life, this day topped the all-time "suck fest" of days for a while. This was my twenty third birthday and I was on my way home from eating lunch. I was waiting for a car to turn and a truck not paying attention hit my car. Since I had watched him in my rear view mirror, I saw him coming and tensed up. Of course I now know that tensing up was a mistake, but it was my reaction. As the truck slammed into my car, I suffered severe muscle damage. My neck was thrown to actually curve opposite of what it should; not only did my neck flatten, but it also went the opposite direction. To this day, I still have a lot of pain due to this accident. I am blessed it was not more serious, but it did definitely put a damper on my "escape this town" route.

This accident caused me to stay in the town I had been living in because my medical care was there, and the doctors that I had were amazing, helpful, and Christians. I really felt like some of them really wanted to get me feeling better rather than just having me spend money. I was upset, I was miserable and in a lot of pain, and I had no idea how this would bring God glory when I sat there barely able to move, having pain so severe that it affected every area of my life. I am sure I was quite unpleasant to be around; I did not mean to complain about the pain in my body, it just seemed to come out of me.

A Miracle in Finances

Now, four years later, I can see a miracle. God used this accident for so many things that have brought him glory. For one, I was advised by a trusted Godly leader to seek the counsel of an attorney. The insurance company refused to pay any of my medical bills, even though that is the purpose of having the insurance, and was just not helpful at all. I prayed and prayed about it, asking for advice from a few Godly leaders. I felt this was the only route that I could take; I did not want to sue the driver or the insurance company. I just wanted my expenses to be taken care of.

After three years of waiting for the settlement to pass, it finally did, but not until the day after I confirmed with Brett that I would be going to Thailand. Count me in; I was going. The day after I committed to the trip, even before we had the dates set, I got a call from my attorney; my settlement was finally going to be approved. I was so elated. He told me what amount of money to expect. Even though it wasn't a lot, it would be enough to allow me to take this trip and cover my medical expenses.

Forming the Team

I am glad that it was not my responsibility to form the team, and I am also really glad and amazed at the way this team turned out. Brett knew that he was taking a team to Thailand at some point in his life, but he didn't know who was on it; I would love to compare notes with him sometime ☺ about his journey of forming the team. I wonder how much he dealt with as he prayed and worked it out with God.

I do know that Brett sent out a lot of invitations to a lot of different people from different crowds and different social groups that he has been part of over the years, and the way that God worked it out was precise. There were a total of 4 of us going from the states, with one member meeting up with us after he finished his outreach portion of school he was doing in Cambodia. The four of us had all previously done ministry together, we knew each other, but we didn't and still don't know everything about each other; it still amazes me that God put these five people together on this trip.

But when do we go?

The first set of dates that we had been looking at included the day of May 22 through sometime in June. By some scheduling conflicts, these dates didn't work for the team to stay full for the whole trip; a member would have to leave early and it just fell through in all regards. The dates of July 11 to July 31 were chosen and we began to pray specifically for what we would be doing as far trip details go; who would fly from what airport and how to get tickets. Finding a time that would work for all of our schedules proved to be a lot more challenging than anyone anticipated. Before the dates were down I had no idea how long our trip would be, and now that this was the middle of the summer, I no longer would be able to get a job due to the time frame of going. I had to trust God to work it all out.

Three weeks. Three full, wonderfully long, beautiful weeks we would be spending in this place I have never been to, never felt called to, and all at once, (I love that I say all at once though it had been months and months and months of praying and seeking and praying some more) I was going to Thailand, to serve God and with some of my favorite people. Amazing!

The crazy thing? Yes, there is more than just the random everything awkwardly falling into place, but again, I "almost didn't get to go". On the original dates of the trip that we had first discussed, the day that we would have been leaving, my father suffered what the doctors believe a mild form of heart attack. Regardless, he had to go through heart surgery, and I would not set foot on that air plane to take me to Thailand if that would have happened. I still have a hard time shaking my head at the specifics!

Crazy "Coincidences"

I'd like to say that the remainder of this school year went smooth with no problems, but that would be incorrect. However, now that I can look back on it, I can again see the hindsight of some of the purposes to the "suck fest" or at least how God worked it into something a little bit magnificent. The timing of conversations and places that they were had all amazed me more and more when I think of it all. The conversation with Brett for instance over the instant messenger happened while I was bored at work. If I hadn't been so fed up with my 'Jungle' household, I would not have sought out something to get me out of that town, some sort of get away. At that time gas was very expensive, so having a job to go to was about the only way I could justify getting out of town. If I hadn't been at a place where my computer was accessible, I would not have had that conversation. I wouldn't have known to keep seeking deeper and deeper to the heart of God.

Soon after I committed to the trip, I received another phone call from my attorney; I would be receiving an extra amount of money, the exact amount of the plane ticket. Wow. Talk about God's confirmation and provision. Can I take a second to point out, I took a step of faith, and committed. Then after I took the step, God provided. I really felt like all the other areas of the trip were set, and that I was to go. Sometimes God requires an act of faith, and act of obedience so we can deepen our level of faith and trust in Him.

God did not have to provide a check for the exact amount of money for the plane ticket; He could have chosen a different way for me to cling to Him and be provided for. There was no way for me to know that would happen; I took a step of faith, followed the Lord, and that is how he confirmed it yet again.

Some instances in my life have required a step of faith without the financial provision to drop into my lap. They have brought me to greater steps of trusting Him. Sometimes, the lack of finances proved to be the closed door on the thing I was praying for and the stepping stone to what was next. I love Him! I love all the ways he goes to measures to gently show us Himself. We must seek and search for him, not His gifting, but His face and heart. He is the one that gives us the gifts, so if we are spending all our time with Him, wouldn't it make sense that he can teach us how to use those very gifting He not only made, but gave us.

I think sometimes it has been proven that we are asked to take a huge step of faith. Even when the arc of the Lord was to cross the Jordan River God had told the priest to put his feet in the water. It was after he had put his feet in the water that the waters not only parted but stood up and made a barrier of water so not only the priest that carried the arc could cross, but the entire nation as well. I can't imagine what it would look like today if they just stood there on the edge of the bank looking at the water waiting for it to do something so they could get across. It was the message from the Lord to get in the river. Sometimes it seems so easy to think of what they did; sure they just stepped in the river, but what about us? How many times have you, have I, stood at the river's edge waiting for the waters to move? (See more about this story in Joshua 3)

Preparation

After this year, I can honestly say my heart was pretty messed up. I felt defeated, I felt flat, and that I was going on this trip broken and wondering what good I would be able to fester up. I knew God was going to have to work a miracle in me while I was there in order to make what I felt to be any sort of impact on the Thai.

In my mind I had a picture of what I would like the preparation for this trip to look like. I wanted to become familiar with the culture; I wanted to begin to learn the language or ways that I could communicate, at least I thought it would sort of look like this. It made sense, right? After all, that is a lot like what Paul, the apostle, did when he would go on trips. He would research the culture and places he was going so he could make the most impact. This was not at all what my preparation looked like. The preparation for this trip was a melting of my heart more and more and being drawn closer to the Lord.

God surprised me. Ha, understatement.(In fact, that was almost a consideration for the title of this book. SUPRIRSE! However, after a conversation with God, basically telling him I was no author, that I was just a girl with a pen… well, you know how that one ended.) That summer I spent a total of 7 days at my house and not all at once either. God sent me on another journey to rediscover some pieces of me that I had forgotten and in the process, a deeper, fuller understanding of Him. I love that there is so much more I have to learn about Him. The more I come to know, the more I know I know nothing at all and the smaller I truly feel. God is so big. I can't comprehend everything at all.

Surprise! Again

I was invited to a retreat hosted by a friend from college that she was having at her house a distance away. I was excited for a time away and hopefully just a time not to be judged so much. I had kind of an idea what this retreat would be like, but really no real expectations, other than that I was supposed to be there. I was also excited because I was now out of the 'jungle'; my lease was over and I was moved into a new place! I knew I was supposed to be there. I had no idea what exactly would happen while there, but I knew I was to be there.

I tried to remain in the back ground and just soak in everything without drawing too much attention to myself. I had just spent a year of my life feeling like I was in the way and told I was anything but holy so I wanted to let God heal me. He did, in of course a crazy ridiculous (marvelous) way. I had told NO ONE of the dreams I had been having, especially the color dreams, the ones that came true. Come on, if no one was going to believe me, and God had given me no reason to share them with these people, why would I have any motivation to become more vulnerable and share?

Then the unexpected happened. The leader came up to me, and specifically asked me about the dreams I had in color. This took me by complete surprise, especially since I hadn't said anything to anyone that was there, about my dreams; in fact, I was doing my best to not talk about them. I have no idea why God chose to have this man ask me about them, but I do know that he wasn't judging and that he also knew about them. It was this gentle prodding that that Lord used to help me remember them, that they are important. With this beginning, my guard began to come down, and this weekend retreat proved to be just the beginning of a crazy restoration process. I can tell you that my heart was pretty heavy; I was hurting and I felt like I had been finally allowed to let my guard down toward God one more time and begin the journey in preparing for Thailand. God did a lot of bringing things back and showing Himself in mighty ways. He did amazing things in all of the hearts of all those present while we were there.

Getting Ready

I tell you, again, that the preparations for Thailand looked nothing like I thought they should. Preparing for a trip overseas I had anticipated that I should spend a lot of time researching the culture in depth, learning the language, trying to find out about the food and get my stomach ready. What God had in mind was a lot different than I anticipated. In fact, it was a journey across the places where He has impacted me. He took me back to Michigan for a few days. While there, I was able to talk to my Pastor and really be honest and open and get some good advice, counsel, and encouragement.

I was also able to study a little of the language, but mainly that trip was to restore parts of me that were broken. I didn't know that at the time, but it was to remind me of who I am in Christ. While there, I spent some time on the shores of Lake Michigan alone and with the Lord. I had my bible, my mp3 player, and a heart that was ready to soak in the King. Sitting at the shores of the lake and even running with the waves in the water, I was reminded again of the powerful blessing it is to be a child of the King.

Even with the blessing of a journey to the shores of Lake Michigan and the life-changing conversations about Jesus with my Pastors from this wonderful part of my life, there were some obstacles that I still had to be overcome. One happened several weeks before my trip to MI, in the last week I was in the 'Jungle' preparing to move to the new house I would be renting. . .

CHAPTER 8

I had been having real trouble being motivated to pack up my house. I was excited to be moving to a new place, a fresh start, but the actual packing, well, it felt like pure torture. I felt like a slug and really couldn't make myself pick the stuff up and put it into the boxes.

To my rescue, my roommate came to my room and suggested we go celebrate the new changes happening in each of our lives and leaving this house. To celebrate, we went to the Chinese restaurant or as I like to call it "to eat China." We enjoyed a nice meal, but I was still heavy- hearted. I suggested we check out the new pet store and hug the puppies.

I am sure to many of you, you are reading my masterful plan, and are already shaking your head. I assure you, this was common practice for me…that is to go to animal shelters or pet stores, hug the puppies, walk them, and play with them, all without collecting a pet. I called it pet therapy; you go and love them while they wait for their adoptive family, and leave them when you leave. It has worked FANTASTIC because I get my animal fix in, a chance to cuddle the puppies and make sure they get some love all without having to take one with me.

This day however, was different. When we went inside the store, all of the puppies were outside in the back of the shop learning the art of going to the bathroom outside. What happened next I could not have seen coming in a million years. From out of nowhere I hear "Diana, this is your puppy,"- Excuse me? I looked around to see if there was anyone around that could have said that. Nope.

My roommate, Tomomi was looking at the fish and no one else was anywhere around, especially one that would know my name. I then look at the puppy board to see what kind of puppies they had. At one point in my life, I had wanted to have a cockapoo (cocker spaniel poodle mix), but the store only had males and I did not want a dog that lifted its leg. I figured I had to be hearing things. So again I hear, "Diana, this is your dog." My immediate thought was, "No way! I do NOT want to clean up his poop and I do NOT want a boy dog."

I then hear my voice asking the clerk to let me see the cockapoo, and again "Diana, this is your dog" I, of course was still arguing with this! I found many reasons why this puppy could not possibly be my dog, I was going to Thailand in a month, school roommates, land lords, time…POOP… and then they bring this little fluffy puppy through the door, just being ever so docile. I was trying to find even more reasons that this puppy could not be mine; he was far too good to be true!

Then they placed this lovely white and tan puppy who seemed to melt in my arms, acting as if there were no place else he were meant to be. I knew at that moment that I had now to find remedies to all those reasons I had just come up with. The voice was even stronger when the puppy was in my arms; I love that God was showing me even before I had seen my little puppy.

Less than 24 hours later, after much prayer to be sure this was really the voice of God, I had made a lot of phone calls to remedy all of those things that I had been fearful of and my reasons why this puppy could not be mine… but it was a very happy morning when I welcomed my Prince Wembley Xavier (Wembley) into my life full time.

Owning a puppy has surprised me in more ways than one. The one that keeps taking me by surprise is how God uses my puppy to show me things about His character and nature and about God's abundant love. Even before Wembley was my dog, that very day, He was teaching me about himself and trusting him. I now see some of you tilting your head thinking I am being whimsical and wondering where on earth I am going with this; I myself often have to shake myself and laugh at how all of this happens.

Some of the lessons came before actually having Wembley, God would ever so gently remind me of them, and then would showing me again when Wembley was mine. Keep in mind any examples that I use I am not referring to myself as perfect; I hope you actually see quite the opposite, see the visual that God used to show me something He's taught me, or is teaching me.

I remember one night last year I was anxious to see God moving in hearts and having them transformed. I was praying and asking God for this, and seeing ways it could possibly happen. My heart just got FULL and I wanted to start RUNNING full speed with all my might after this. Later that night, I imagined a dog on a leash with his master who was walking along their journey together. The puppy then BOLTS and starts running at full speed however the master continues to hold on and keeps walking the speed for their journey. Needless to really say, I am sure when the puppy reached the end of the leash; he could have a pretty sore neck.

I was able to witness my own little puppy taking on some of these very characteristics. Wembley was on a leash outside tied to the house and he saw something and took off running after it. I had given him a pretty long leash that he could run outside with and still be safe in the confines of our yard, so my puppy had some time to pick up speed. Imagine if you will this little fluff ball running full speed coming to the end of his rope. I tried to stop him so he wouldn't hurt himself, but it didn't work. When he ran as far as his leash would allow, my little puppy managed to become an acrobat. I think he mastered the back flip somersault that day, and thinking back makes me think of the pain his neck wouldn't have had to endure…

I also began thinking along the lines of walking with puppies when taking them for a walk. I am not really sure what had my mind thinking so much about puppies before I actually had one, but I believe it must have been God preparing to teach me and show me something I can relate to. Anyway, I had a visual image of a timid puppy, being nervous and not really walking along side of his master, really being drug along and not cooperating, not really out of pure disobedience, but one of extreme caution. Imagine if you will a strong willed puppy just scared and not wanting to go along with you, when the destination is going to be somewhere great!

I again experienced this when I had Wembley. This pup is an adventurous hearted puppy, but still has his moments of extreme timidity and caution and is not so fun to take for a walk when he doesn't want to walk with me. Either extreme is very difficult to walk with him. It is much easier when he walks along side of me. I give him some extra rope to explore, sniff and see things along the way, but generally speaking, it is a nicer walk when he isn't pulling in both directions on his leash.

Now of course, this isn't a perfect picture of our lives with God; HE does not have us on a leash with our walk with him. Think about it in this way: I know that when I get excited and run ahead of God without really asking if we are running at this together or if he has shown me something, I just get super excited. If I get freaked out and am not really sure what we are doing, I start to drag my heels. I just see that walking with God is the best way possible. Obviously that seems like an easy lesson to do," Why, yes, I am going to walk along side of God," but these visuals really helped me see the differences that we can do in our lives. I know that God loves running after those things with me. He likes to take us to new places in our lives, to explore, be curious, and get us excited. He likes to show us things because He loves us. He likes to walk with his children, beside us and making the path for our feet to walk upon and I think he also uses this to teach us His timing.

Timing is everything. Have you ever crossed a road with a puppy? That little guy is generally so excited to just keep moving and see what is on that other side and is FIXED on getting there, that he doesn't see the possible dangers (aka CARS) that await or other things to wait for (other people coming along.) Timing is everything when walking with puppies! Or that lovely time when Wembley decides he must go to the bathroom in the MIDDLE of the road and you have to make him move right now or that car that came from nowhere will hit him! We may see something up ahead that we want to chase, have been given a clear picture of and we want to go chase it right now, but we don't see the whole picture sometimes. Sometimes we want to wait a little longer, but it is the time to go right now. I know that when Wembley and I reach a corner he sometimes wants to fly across the road and I pull back on his leash. He will now at least look to me and wonder what I have pulled back on his leash for. I wonder how often we do this with God…

I also think of my training with Wembley. I remember sitting with him on the kitchen floor trying to teach him how to sit up. He would look at me like I was the craziest being in the entire world, with that "You want me to do what?" look on his face. He would look with determination, trying to figure out what on earth I was asking of him and hold up a paw. When he didn't understand how to get the treat I was giving him as an incentive, he looked so discouraged. He would wiggle and waggle but still looked confused and he kept trying. All the while I was never angry or frustrated at my pup for not being able to do what I was teaching him. I was just patiently teaching him, redoing it and going through the process that he needed in order to be able to successfully achieve the task we were working on.

Never once did I expect him to learn this without my assistance or teaching. Watching him as he tried to learn was a joy to me. He would look so frustrated and look like he had disappointed me by the way his puppy face would react when he didn't get his treat. He didn't disappoint me; I knew we were in this process together, and this picture doesn't entirely work for God, because I am SOOO not the perfect teacher. Wembley would want his puppy treat right away, the first time, but it was in the doing and the failing that is now how he has been able to learn. Wembley is now a pro at sit up, shake, hold hands, sit, roll over and dance…

When I watched Wembley attempting to do what I am sure he felt impossible, I was so happy that he was attempting the task I was asking. I knew it would take time, but I also knew it could be done . . . sort of how God asks me to do a task that seems impossible! I almost always go into that "Um, was that God?" mode instead of just looking to him and seeing that He is going to guide me in the steps that it takes to complete the process it takes to do this. Be honest. Have you gone to this mode, the freak out mode immediately to then breathe and then look to God? I know I have.

God reminds me of this frequently and has begun to change my perspective to not go quite to freak out mode and here I see my failures or inability and immediately want to give up. God is faithfully pursuing us to keep going. We are learning and growing and are not expected to be perfect. Here is where God constantly reminds us that He is in control, He will provide for what He has asked of us, will ask us to give up some things that seem impossible, but all in all, it brings us closer to Him and his heart.

I think the most tangible expression God has shown me in having Wembley is the concept of true unconditional love. This is a concept I've wrapped my mind around, embraced, but in having a puppy God has truly given me a glimpse of this and if I get to see all of this with a puppy, then I can't wait to be a parent. . .

Let me clarify a little to tell you what I mean how God has shown me this. I look at my cute little fluffy ball of dog and can't help but have my heart get a little soft, but that isn't exactly the love I am talking about. My puppy is in no way perfect, and the guys at the HT or the girls at the Pearl could certainly testify to that. They were the wonderful houses full of people that watched my dog during another adventure that I'll mention later in this story. Yet it is even in his messes, his accidents of poop on the floor (which surprisingly he doesn't do for me) and times where he disobeys me that I am fully committed.

I love him and because of that, I will take care of him and look after him, and even that falls short of a description of perfect unconditional love, because I am a human and I have had to leave Wembley behind but I have always made sure he is looked after and cared for. I am flawed in this area because of my limitations, but I am committed. Not just my actions, but seeing this puppy that comes and greets me no matter what I have done, who is happy to see me wagging his tail, I can feel his love for me. It is great, I don't have to give him anything for that love - he just does.

There is something so wonderful about the way a puppy loves his master and I feel God in that too, by letting the calluses around my heart melt a little bit more. I have this creature that doesn't see my flaws or my imperfections, coming up with reasons why he shouldn't or should love me; he just does with no reservations. He welcomes me when I come home and is always happy to see me and to my dismay, full of sloppy, wet puppy kisses.

Just recently, I have been having a difficult time where I have been struck with feelings of terrible inadequacy and loneliness, really wanting to spend some quality time with God. I would spend my time with my friends who know the Lord and have some fellowship; I mean how can you go wrong? I was at a lock-in inside a church, where surprisingly they let my Wembley come along inside. Dealing with myself I wanted to be around these people, but my heart was hurting, something was missing that I desperately needed.

I sat down at the piano and another girl was playing. Wembley was being played with. He was being well cared for and entertained, in fact I felt quite content watching him play with the others. He went and had his time with people that knew me and that he had been acquainted with. Then something remarkable happened. The entire rest of the people began to play hide and seek in the dark, leaving me in this large area, with a piano, and the lights off. Oh my dearest heart content! I had a piano to sing my prayers and praises to the Lord. I feel I can express myself the best when I sing my heart to the Lord when no one is watching.

I thought to myself that Wembley would probably go run around all these people and follow them around while they played in the church. After all, they were moving about and he likes to play. What I encountered was the exact opposite and the most wonderful blessing the Lord in what HE showed me through it.

So as I sat there at this piano, praying my guts out in the form of singing as loud and passionate as possible, and my dog sat at my feet. Here he had the reign over the entire place, he had the choice to go and play with anyone and spend time with anyone there, and yet, he just sat at my feet. Now, I am not sure exactly when this radical discovery happened, or how I haven't really seen it, because I know I need time alone with God, my master, but seeing my dog there, just sitting at my feet regardless of me, just to spend time with me. I was humbly reminded of the beauty of it all. I just want to sit at the feet of my master, and soak him in. After I get to spend time at the feet of the cross, sitting there with my master, no expectations from him, but just sitting with him, soaking in His goodness, singing, or talking or listening, or reading, it is just so good. I am a much better person to be around anyway.

Regardless of the stresses of this world, I desperately need time to be with my king. I love that God showed me this with my little dog sitting at my feet. How simple a lesson that I probably was going to overlook, yet God blessed me with being able to see this with the love my dog has for me, and I am such an imperfect human,

I make mistakes I hurt people that I don't want to hurt, and how much more then can it be for God! He loves me, and I get to love Him in his perfection. In His goodness, in just Him being Him, fully being loved is truly a mysterious thing.

A few days ago, I was getting ready to leave, and I was taking Wembley with me. I put on my jacket, which immediately sent him in a hyper ecstatic mode. He is dancing and jumping and running frantic to and fro. He began jumping at the door and was just thrilled looking, trying to get his leash off the wall and everything. When I put him on his leash to go outside, he just could barely contain his excitement. The thought that ran through my head was he had no idea where we were going! It wasn't going to be an exciting car ride, I think it was just to go to the grocery store, but it didn't matter where we were going, what we were doing, he was just excited to be going along with his master. BOOM! Wait.

I know that I have had moments like this, where the unknown adventure with God seems to be so exciting and I can't wait to go along with him just to see what He has planned, what the course seems to be. I know that I struggle with having that excitement all the time, the what-ifs plague me. I want to move past the what-ifs and have that kind of enthusiasm when with the King, that I don't care where we are going, what we are doing, as long as I have God right beside me, it is exactly where I should go and where I should be. Sometimes I get restless; I want to know where we are going, what we are doing!

I love the way how God just gives a tangible or visible picture in the craziest of ways, and it is not always that it is a brand new idea or thought, but just another expression of his love for us. It is not just that I had never known about these things, or that I hadn't known of, it is just the really big God who loves to surprise His children. He always loves us, always cares for us, and I am grateful to have Wembley.

CHAPTER 9

I learned quickly in Thailand that there were some very simple elements that I take for granted of having an abundant supply of. The one element of my "normal" existence is the presence of toilet paper. It is not really something that I think about just in my everyday thoughts; it's just one of those things when using the facilities that just should be there. I had managed to find most Western-style toilets to do my business in, and the beginning of the trip had a plentiful supply.

When we were in Pattaya, my first encounter with a hose and a bucket replaced that blessed paper. It was there after I had done what I needed to do, that instead of toilet paper, I was staring into the face of this hose and bucket, not even sure the correct way that it worked. I won't go into any more detail, but I realized then even though I had traveled and had tried to have some sort of idea of what this trip would look like, that I was in for a lot of stepping out of my comfort zone, and even going a step beyond that. I hadn't even got to the squatty potties. Those scared me; I was afraid to fall in. Again, more stories that I won't try to paint images in your head. This was just a layer of what I thought "breaking my comfort zone" was.

I have felt that I get along pretty easily wherever I go. I have traveled before and have lived in many different living situations, so I just anticipated the most awkward situations. Even after I did this, I found that Thailand wasn't even close. I love how God takes my ideas and shows his spirit in them. You may wonder what spiritual connection I was gaining from this whole not wanting to fall into the toilet ordeal, but this was just the beginning of ruining in the best way, my ideas of this trip, letting God completely do his good thing and break my ideas of what ministry should look like. When you are uncomfortable, you can either cling to what you do have of comfort, or take that step and embrace those uncertain moments and cling to the only one worth clinging to: Jesus Christ.

What Man May See

Sometimes, I firmly believe that God wants to know how foolish we are willing to look for him. If we are willing to overstep what seems normal, to see if we are going to follow him, we can overstep those cultural and social boundaries that we place on Him. It may be to take away the images that we put in our minds of the years of tradition that have transpired, not that they have been wrong, but maybe it could just be to expand on our understanding and friendship with our King. He tests our faithfulness. He didn't just stop asking us to do things that may seem outrageous in Genesis, asking Abraham to sacrifice the promised son as well as providing Abraham with descendants as great as the stars in the sky. God was allowed to provide that day! I wonder how many Abraham/Isaac situations I have missed because I was afraid to give up the thing I thought God had promised. How many have you?

The more I grow, the more I see opportunities to have God receive greater glory from our obedience, even if it looks ridiculous to mans' eyes. The beautiful thing is, it generally isn't even about the "ridiculous" thing we have been asked to do; it is about the willingness to follow Him. I will share so many experiences in this that may make you laugh, but it is so true. This experience I am drawn remember is again, about my spiritual brother and friend Steve with the story I am about to share.

I will do my best to recall this as best as I can. I am not Steve, and even to clarify will be difficult because he is in a different country than I am, but I will give the best account of what I remember. Even before Steve had got his guitar, he had been continually praying for what he was to do with his next step and how China fit into that. He was praying about going there for another opportunity to share the Lord.

It was with some creative-type of ministry through the arts with some of his friends and still didn't know HOW he was going to get there, where the money was going to come from for the plane ticket, and again, there was the ever pressing issue of a visa. Visas for China can be extremely difficult to obtain, especially for the purpose of sharing the Lord, and going about it in an honest and legitimate way.

So Steve knew he was going to need a visa, and he had been praying about it. Even before he had his guitar, he had a vision to go to the China embassy with his guitar attached to his back, and that is what he knew.

He had no paperwork, and he also knew that if he were granted the visa, it was what God wanted. It was beautiful and terrifying obedience, knowing that it wasn't about going to get the visa, it was about Jesus. "It's all about Jesus," Steve always says. If he got the visa, that was extra bonus, and if not, he stepped out of what made sense, out into bold faith of willingness of looking crazy, being made fun of, and scorned by the dudes at the embassy…to do what is crazy. Now that is Jesus!

When we can wrap our minds around the fact that everything is about Jesus, the tasks at hand do not need to make sense. Sometimes it is extremely frustrating when we think we have followed so closely and find we haven't reached the thing asked of us. Or sometimes we are asked to let go of a promise, only to receive it back after we have given it up or we are asked to give it up and never get it back; it can be so frustrating! I am dealing with working this out right now with the Lord and I haven't a clue on it all. I just am trying to not hold tightly to things and trust God in His amazing will. He has a plan that goes beyond and can take the worst things and make them beautiful.

Steve didn't get his visa that day, (though he did eventually get it a few days later) but the Lord grated him the most unique day. It happened to be some random Chinese holiday where the Embassy was closed so he wasn't able to get his visa. He did get three splendid hours with his guitar, singing his guts out, praying and worshiping the love of his life on the stairs of the Chinese Embassy in the middle of Thailand. It was all about Jesus! Let's talk about bringing worship to the Nations. . .

Child-Like Faith

There is something inspiring about a child and the innocence and purity they bring to a group of people. The way they are in awe, wonder, are curious and just delightful to be around, something that brings a level of peace, untainted, unbiased. The Thai believers reminded me of such wonderfulness. I remember in Pattaya, playing a game for hours that consisted of simply a blanket and two teams of people sitting behind them. Players pick a person on either team and have to the count of three when the blanket is quickly dropped. The team that says the name of who is on the other side of the blanket wins. HOURS of this game, hours of enjoyment, simple fun.

Being in Thailand, I saw how God was transforming these peoples' lives. Before any sort of legalism could set in, they didn't know the ins and outs, they just knew that there was a God that just radically changed their lives, and that they would be forever changed! Hallelujah! If I could even begin to address how they worshiped, if you could see the expressions on their faces, the pure love they experienced for their savior.

If I could help you feel a feeling simply through the reading of these words, I'd do that. Overwhelming pure unhindered love for their King was just oozing out of them. With no worries of what anyone else was doing, or saying, just loving their King, singing, dancing, sitting, whatever they needed to do to tell their King what they felt for him, expressing their gratitude; yeah, I don't have enough words, and even the pictures I took, wouldn't do it justice. It was amazing. I've seen such pure worship little times in my life, not that it is less… but such innocence.

I think the innocence also is an essence of the things that have been overcome. When someone is set free from something that consumes them, living in the freedom and following of Christ is an amazing thing. Yes, we have our cross to carry, but we have a savior that has died for our sins and WE GET TO LIVE FOR HIM. He gives us the biggest purpose in the entire world. The fact that Christ loves us so much, that he doesn't live or reside inside of a gold statue, but gives us a purpose for life (glorifying him) is so incredibly amazing!… I don't know about you but it is so very awesome to have purpose in life again.

When these new believers saw the light that Jesus had spoken and the light reflecting off the others, their hearts were curious. The Holy Spirit opened their hearts, and they were set free. Their lives had not magically been taken out of the slums, but they were given a hope and life to follow that hope.

It isn't about the stuff we have; it isn't about how much we don't have- it is about Jesus. Innocence. I was able to witness new life in Thailand; I saw the minds grasp something I so often can forget with the struggles and just trying to make it. There are so many pressures here in the States; having to have and hold a job, make money, there are far more bills here, and just everything of maintaining life; we forget about the innocence of our first love.

Dancing In The Rain

We had gone to the Thai market and had our senses stimulated by the intense arrangement of items. Such a vast array of supplies, crafts and art from the Thai expanding as far as the eye could see. It was such a crazy experience, much larger and more exciting than any mall I can imagine. I am not the best shopper; I get bored of seeing things that I could never afford, or things that look just like everything else that I just came in contact with. I get overwhelmed with the amount of STUFFness that is there. This however, was a different experience. First of all, the culture instilled in the streets of this HUGE outdoor market goes beyond what words I am capable of describing. It was better than any American fair that I have ever been at, or heard of. It still amazes me, trying to remember it, the scents, the dust, the variety of people, the variety of stories instilled in their materials, the food we ate. Mangos on sweet rice, I think? I don't even know. . .

Leaving the market, we hailed a taxi to take us to the next place on our stop which was to the other side of town to go to church for the evening. Riding in a taxi in Thailand means putting your life inside a colorful car driven by a fairly experienced driver, but it is an amazingly scary time. These cars are zooming in and out of traffic, squeezing in places that you are certain you are going to break the door off, or for sure the mirrors. You are left to wonder why there are not cushions to ensure your safety as you zoom by things on the opposite side of the road. Not only this, but fitted are six people in a space designed for four. I've been in a taxi in the States in some larger cities such as New York but nothing compared to the rides we took in Thailand.

That evening, church was a powerful service I was fortunate enough to witness some people that didn't know God still worship Him. This was probably the most incredible time I have ever been part of because it was more than just singing. I saw a difference in the eyes and the way the faces of worshippers was different than a person that was just singing. A person singing from the heart to the Lord (the thing that we were created to do) simply radiates a glow from within. I love also how scripture tells us that if we don't worship the creator, even the rocks will cry out… I want to be the one crying out in love and adoration to my King, not the rocks. This service brought me to a new level of adoration and passion and love for my King, to see him working in the hearts of those that didn't know him, yet it being evident at the same time.

After church, there were about eleven of us that went out for a special treat… milk! In Thailand, milk is a special treat. It is not readily available, but it comes in about a thousand different flavors and varieties; strawberry, blueberry, pineapple, caramel, the list goes on and on. The rain was pouring down outside, pitter patter dancing across the pavement and sidewalks, echoing their joyous melodies. The drops cascaded from the sky and touched everything in sight. Nothing was left unsaturated and I couldn't with hold any more. My heart was also bursting with joy and there was nothing that could stop me. I grabbed my friend Tukta and we flew out the door and began twirling and dancing and laughing in the street. I am fairly positive that Tukta thought I was crazy, but she was smiling and laughing, probably at me. I loved dancing in the rain. She went inside and I grabbed Nida and we too, danced and twirled in the raining streets.

While dancing in the streets, God spoke to me even more. He is like the rain; his presence is everywhere and there isn't anything that is absent from his touch. The sounds of the rain, the overwhelming patter of the drops pouring on the ground, and the unquenchable outpouring from the sky; it was as if the heavens had just opened and drenched the earth with its needed water. Only Jesus is the unending fountain of life, the living water; so much better! I want to remember that if I should ever become overwhelmed again. I like Psalm 42, especially verse 7 where it says, "Deep calls to deep in the roar of your waterfalls; all your waves and breakers have swept over me." The water, the rain, and the awareness of his presence of the Lord can be like a mighty waterfall.

I know I am so overwhelmed and humbled by Him, yet He is completely gentle, He is so powerful, so loving, so huge, yet we can sit inside and not even notice Him, just like the rain. God's presence is intimate and He has the complete ability to drench us with His love, his grace, and His mercy because he loves us. I want to be drenched in that rain so that I can radiate and reflect his goodness and light off of me so others can be just as saturated by the Lord. His voice is like the rain, it nurtures our souls, it is essential for life; without it we would die. I want to be drenched in the love of the Lord and be reminded of it, to be dancing in the rain of Jesus every day, not to stay inside in fear, or to use an umbrella to keep him off of me. He is unquenchable and I need Him. I can't live without him in my life.

I realize in everyday life, there may be times I may have to use an umbrella or even stay inside, but with Jesus, I never want to limit Him to the condition of the storm in my life; I want His presence to be overcoming my soul all the time. I am so desperate for Him and his rain in my life, His unquenchable living water to be in my soul all the time. He is all that hope comes from, He is everything. I wish it was raining right now, even though the water would be freezing since it is winter in Wisconsin, but I want to go out and be drenched in the rain and a reminder, but even more, to go and be drenched in the love of Jesus.

CHAPTER 10

Sometimes when I write this story and recall the events and things I tell you, it sometimes is hard to remember that it was me that did all these things. It is so easy when life throws all these crazy things around you to forget; forget the memories, the fragrances, the textures, the humidity, the emotions…

Lord, my fingers are at your mercy. I so badly want to recall all that you have me to recall, to write this book to bring you glory and to set the captive heart free. Lord, my heart right now even feels captive. Please free me enough to write, to remember all that you have done, Lord, an Ebenezer (this is a place of significance and a reminder of what the Lord has done. In the Old Testament they used to build altars to be able to go back to where God had done something)**, help me remember. Lord you are good, and I don't want to be as forgetful as the people in Ezekiel. Please control my fingers and let them go where you want them to go.**

Jubilee

I looked back over my journal entries and my online posts when I was in Thailand to spark some memory and some inspiration to remember. I still love Thailand and their shoeless policy. I am sure I have already mentioned this, but I love being barefoot! It is freeing! I know that in Thailand it is a cultural thing that the feet are the most disrespectful part of the body, but that meant for me freedom for my feet! Most store fronts and the internet cafes where we spent our time communicating to the people of the states and just updating on our adventures, all had a lovely pile of shoes outside the door. Yes, freedom! My feet were not confined!

On one particular day when we walked into BJD,(this is the place where we stayed, and it is a large dorm like building that focuses on God for the students that stay there) the floor not only had a pile of shoes at the door, but they were spread out in a vast selection of colors, smells, and textures. There was also a symphony of laughing, smiling people sitting on colorful floor covering.

All around me, there were people preparing mountains of food. To the right of me at least three blanket-sized coverings were filled with bowls of vegetables that were being chopped, cut and washed, prepared to be cooked. Next to them were the vegetables that had been cooked and prepared, waiting to be served. In the next room over, bustling people were coming and going, scouting out the area to find unique things that could be used to decorate. In the back corner were blades of grass that were taller than I am tall. They were thicker than any blade of grass I have ever seen, coming in by armful bundles, waiting to be washed, wiped and freed from insects. In the front of these magnificent blades, the colorful ribbons that had been collected from the market were adorned. There were people and things everywhere for the preparations. For what you ask? A celebration. What kind of celebration? A jubilee celebration, one of redemption, and freedom from debt was about to happen.

After I spent about two hours wiping these extremely tall blades of grass, I went with Brandon to the slums to pick up some of the people, including Yai Noy, who I mentioned earlier in the story. Being able to go with Brandon and pick up the people that I felt so honored to share in this special celebration was such a privilege to me. That is something I treasure, and want to be able to endorse it in my life. I know I am not perfect, but I strive to be able to drop things and invite people to live life along side of me, this was another chance at that.

Sometimes I am still surprised that we were allowed to take part in this special celebration. I got to see people who have been part of this ministry, and God blessed me to be there at the exact moment to experience the end result of years and years of praying, seeking, and to see the answer. Their building was paid for. I don't know if this resonates deep inside of you or not, but for me, it brings me shivers. Here is a building that houses so many people.

Not only is it a shelter, this building allows the space to be able to provide training, love and hope to echo through the walls. In these walls many lives are weaved together for a period of time, and I can tell you that in my brief three weeks there, it had changed my life. It of course, isn't the building itself, but God almighty, providing for it all! This right now even encourages me. Often times we are at the start of something or at the middle or even the "weeding" process of something so to witness a "harvest" or an answered prayer is a blessing and honor. Being able to share it with Yai Noy and my other new friends that I met made it so much richer.

As we pulled back up to the building, we heard the music fill the street, people spilling out of the warehouse doors that surrounded the first floor. So many lives were represented in that small space. We ate, we prayed, we sang, and we danced. I sit here and smile as I remember dancing, completely undignified, excited and happy. No words or language stood between us. We didn't need those to communicate our gratitude and thankfulness to the King.

Thinking about this now makes me want with all I have deep within my soul to celebrate when someone comes to know the freedom of Christ living in them. The freedom and redemption Jesus offers. Oh how I want to dance for their freedom. I want to run around skipping jubilantly in my yard with my hands in the air and my heart on fire. Another person knows the peace of knowing that eternity is theirs with Christ! Oh the blessed freedom! In fact, I think I will go and dance, in anticipation of what is left to come. . . .

Orange Juice

I love orange juice. Real orange juice, the kind made from that wonderful sweet fruit that is orange and sweet and tangy… mmmm! I am not sure when exactly it started, but one day I wanted orange juice so bad. So, since there was a plethora of stores around that sold different types of juice and other drinks, I didn't think it would be a challenge. I of course, was wrong. There were substitutes, and some got close, but nothing compared to the real deal. This became a new thing for me to pursue while in Thailand, as silly as it sounds, pursuing the perfect orange juice. That night after the party was no exception. We went to the night market to wander around and take a glance at what was out that night.

I know it sounds a little funny, that I have an entire section of this story dedicated to orange juice, but it was more than just the pursuit of orange juice, I wanted the real thing, something to quench my thirst for orange juice. Jesus, he is the real thing, and just like the orange juice is the only thing that would satisfy my urge for the juice, Jesus is the only thing that can ever satisfy the eternal thirst in our soul. I think sometimes we forget about Jesus, or we stop craving him when things get boring, or when things get ridiculously difficult. We instead settle for tangerine, or apple, but what we really want is orange juice, what we really need is Jesus. We need him, not just talking about him, or talking to others about him, but HIM, deep and rich, intimately meeting with him every moment of our lives.

He is right here with us, our lives can never been the same, even when we are bored, or discouraged, they aren't the same. I want Jesus so much more than I wanted that orange juice, and well, while I was there, I tried a lot of types of juice. I found some that would taste ok, even some that didn't taste too bad, but none substituted for the real thing. I didn't go out of my way every day, but it was in the back of my mind most of the time, and if I am willing to seek orange juice, oh I want to be so much more willing to seek God and His face. I don't want to run into things that hurt, but I am afraid that seems to be part of this journey, and seeking him out.

Lord, I seek you in this journey of remembering. Please guide my fingers across the pages and let what you would, sing out across the pages.

That night, at least I am pretty sure it was that night, I had a dream. The night I had the dream doesn't matter, but the dream itself does. The dream was a preview, I didn't really understand, but I awoke knowing it was significant again. I sometimes wish I could describe to you the difference in a dream I just dream that my imagination creates—one that is simply my subconscious providing entertainment-- versus the ones that I know mean something more.

The thing I remember most about this dream was going to visit Steve in Canada. I would stand along the side of a stream, and God would tell me what to do once I got there. I woke up feeling a little sad; a few days earlier I had gone along to the airport to bid Steve farewell as he set out to Korea and then on to China. I was privileged to be able to pray for and send this new friend off into the next adventure that God had called him to, but almost devastated that it may be a forever goodbye. Steve had jokingly suggested coming and visiting someday, only I didn't know WHERE that even would be!

The night before Steve left, several of us farangs (foreigners) got together in our room and sang our hearts and love out to the One we have in common: the beautiful Savior Jesus, the One that brought us all to Thailand at the same time, the One that unites, the ONE. Not one of us was born in Thailand, yet our hearts were now tied here to these people, and to each other. As we sang and worshiped, I remember the same feeling I am feeling right this very moment- how life entangles us in it, how much you can love when you are allowed, how beautiful it is to worship so freely with people you have just met. Since the bond of Christ seems to be the strongest one I know, being able to intimately worship alongside of each other, it is crazy to imagine that here on this earth, they may only be physically present for a small while, but forever leave an imprint on your being. The best assurance is knowing one day I will get to sit with so many wonderful people and sing songs to the King forever. Eternity. Sigh.

Lord, you know my heart; you know what it feels inside. Why is it such a struggle to write today, why does my heart ache so much today? How can I turn these into passions scribed out on the pages this reader touches?

Not everything went perfectly.

I have written about so many wonderful things about Thailand, but I can't let you think everything was perfect. We are imperfect people trying to share the life of a perfect Savior. It is impossible for us to be perfect; we make mistakes, we hurt people and we get hurt. I know most of the hurt is unintentional, while unfortunately, some of that will be intentional.

Unity is always a difficult thing. We crave it and try to facilitate opportunities for it, yet sometimes by choice, or oblivion we are the very essence of disunity. One of the not so perfect moments was a time when there was an accidental time of disunity, a miscommunication, and trying so hard to fit within boundaries, left some very hurt feelings. I don't want to focus on that; I would much rather talk about the joys, but in the midst of joys are struggles, discouragements and heartache.

Lord, I am at the mercy of whatever you can have me type, I feel like you have granted me an amazing thing and privilege to be allowed to share what you have shown me and taught me and allowed me to love through.

Struggle

This may seem strangely misplaced in the telling of the story, but I feel you should know how the process of me actually writing this story is going. It is terribly frightening and difficult on most days. I get so excited to be able to tell the memories, the stories, the things God allowed me to see, yet I get flustered; it's like my fingers get all tangled up in a mess.

This season of my life will be the next book I write, so I won't go into great details now, but I can't go any further without these things pouring out of my fingers. It seems everything is preventing me from writing and remembering and retelling the story that God has gifted me with. I was thinking of a passage in Mark that talks about sharing and telling. I was encouraged through this struggle of even the purpose in me writing this story. We are told so many times in the Bible to tell it, tell it, tell what God has done, tell what He is doing, and tell his story. This very moment I did a search online at a trusted Bible reference site and there are a crazy amount of times we are told to tell. The specific reference I am talking about is Mark 5:9. After this man had been freed from demon possession, he was told to go home and tell everyone the wonderful things God had done, and how merciful he had been. How exciting of a task! To tell what God has done!

This is limitless. Though it has been a struggle for the words, the emotions, and the remembrance of the passion that God gives, He encouraged me this very moment. God didn't just do things then, He still does them. In so many ways beyond our finances, but in sharing our lives with others, we get to take part in his master plan, and we can tell others about it. The manner in which we can share it can affect how it is told, but sometimes in sharing our story, or even better hearing out someone's story, we get to share and receive blessings, encouragement, perspective like you wouldn't believe.

In writing this, it encourages me to know, that my three weeks in Thailand, and the rest of this story, has this super cool chance to live on and not only have the impact last those three weeks, but possibly a lot longer if anyone else can be encouraged by the words that spin across this page. I am not saying everyone will be required to write a book, or give speeches, but be willing to be vulnerable to share what God has done. It is our story and His story blended. We get to share how we messed up, to grow from it and walk along someone else that finds themselves in the same situations. We can also just help someone reach up to heaven, getting to share when we succeed. It all should point us back to God and our utter need and dependence on Him! He is mighty, that is for sure.

I am excited for the possibilities that come forward. I have no idea what the Lord will have my life look like for the remaining days and years I have left. I do know, that no matter my struggle, no matter how hard it gets, I want to follow and chase God with all that I have inside of me. I have a hard time remembering sometimes, and I am blessed to be allowed the ability to put my experience into words. It makes my mind swim a little. It's kind of exciting and I know moving on from here is possible in this story, I know that it can be done. That also brings great encouragement to be able to continue on outside of writing this. So, with that brief interruption and detour, here comes the rest. . .

CHAPTER 11

We sat at a bus station at two in the morning on the other side of the world looking rather ragged. Our hair was in disarray, and well, after several hours of travel, you may imagine the fragrance, err, odor we were wearing. Some of us managed to get a few moments rest on the journey. I never thought I'd be there, but then again, not much seems to go the way I think it should, and yet the Lord worked it out beautifully. As we sat there, the six of us plus two of our Thai friends, in this tiny, sort of sketchy bus station, we awaited the next part of our journey in Thailand to unfold before us.

The time was getting short that we'd be able to stay in Thailand, but the adventure was far from over. The ride to this station had even been an amazing adventure, for me anyway. I was blessed listening to life stories and insights of Jesus through messages given by other lovers of Him.

Shortly after 2 AM, the person coming to collect us arrived. Our bus had arrived ahead of schedule so we had a little time to wait and rest. It was sort of nice to take a moment to regroup and try to collect the thoughts dancing around in our head. I was so excited for this portion of our trip. It had been something we solidly knew would happen before we even left the soil of the United States; we were headed north to the visit the orphans.

We gathered our belongings and the items we brought along and climbed into the back of a pickup sungtow (remember this is a truck with benches in the back that acts as a mode of transportation). I am not sure how long it took us to arrive at our next destination, but I was certainly glad we had our Thai friends Tee and Tukta with us. When we arrived to the facility that houses and cares for about fourteen abandoned children and we spilled ourselves out of the sungtow. Groggily we followed this driver and head leader of the facility to the space we would sleep for the next few hours.

I am not sure how to accurately describe this place we slept in, but I will again do my best to attempt to conquer the task of trying to bring you to the place where I was so you too can experience it. This room was tiny; smaller than 5 feet by 6 feet with a very small window. The floor was concrete covered in some tiles. There were to be four of us women staying in this space. Writing this, I got the chance to look back over my last year. This was probably one of my favorite nights sleeping in Thailand. Even though it was so small and so out of the ordinary, they found a place for us to sleep!

This room was snug, (we slept like sardines in a can) but I knew that my closeness to the person next to me was going to be worth it when I woke up and saw the children and got to see what God was going to do in this very place! Somehow the close quarters didn't matter to me. I can't say what the others in the group thought, or what the expectations were, but I felt like one of the people.

Lord, here we are again, writing these things, remembering all that you have done. I look and am reminded of my dear friend

Tukta, Lord! How much of a blessing it is to know that we got to be there with Tukta and see her come through and come to know you! Thank you Lord for taking her and loving her and for allowing her to know you! You are powerful and almighty and your mercy never ends. Father, you love us so much! Please Lord, guide my fingers, and please help me remember what you did, and what you are still doing, and what you allowed us to be part of. Thank you for a glimpse of the bigger picture and how even a short trip of three weeks can make for your eternal glory. Father, help my mind be fixed on you. I adore you and I need you to guide my fingers. Where do I go from here?

The first night there in the midst of the darkness I awoke and had to use the bathroom. Carefully attempting to reach the door just feet from me was rather a challenge, trying to dodge the limbs of my friends. I felt like I had accomplished the impossible when I exited the room. Little did I know I was about to encounter my first experience with a squatty potty. Next to our room was a beautiful bathroom with a western-style toilet. I was excited to see that. It was my secret ambition to NOT use a squatty potty while I was in Thailand. I am not sure why, but they intimidated me!

All the things that can go wrong while using the other style toilet were constant reasons why I wanted to avoid them, and for almost three weeks I had; that is, until this moment. The western-style toilet was not working; I would have to brave the unknown, again. I won't go into any more details, but I will say it was a successful trip that I did NOT fall in.

The next morning I remember ants. I am not sure what treats I had stowed away in my bag, but the ants were on a mission to find them and invaded our space. They had found their way over my feet and had begun a conquest up my leg. I was literally tickled awake by these tiny black creatures scurrying around my body. The sun had begun to shine through the window, and I was excited to start the day and to meet with the children. They had went to school for the day but we got to tour the place that they called home.

It is hard for me to imagine that just five years before it was a building, it was just trees. Now, it has a solid foundation of bricks, stones and cement! God is great! There are two dorms, if you can envision. One was for girls that hosted four bunk beds with some mattresses pushed up against the wall for them to sleep on at night. The boys' dorm had four bunk beds as well. I know they work hard at keeping this place. The cleanliness of the building and the comfort of the facility was a blessing from God.

We spent that day getting familiar with the leaders. I really feel a special bond for one of the leaders, my friend Hannah. My heart smiles right now as I think about that first day as she shared her story with me, as well as the stories of how God has used their ministry to provide for the basics of these children that have the unfortunate status of being abandoned. Thai law prevents most adoptions for abandoned or refuge children so it is a miracle that this place was able to exist and provide shelter, care, and LOVE for these children. We also were blessed with being able to see the means in which this whole operation is funded and supported by making the most beautiful handmade greeting cards.

~~~****~~~

The walls were made of boards, and not the boards like we find in America; these boards were thin and bent. The floors were made out of posters and wafer or other thin boards with gaps in between them. They were crafted skillfully together with duct tape and tacks, allowing for holes and gaps where bugs and animals have
~~~

easy access. There was canvas on the walls, not covering them completely, but it helped to give them more of a wall feel.

There was also no furniture, just thin mats to sleep on the floor, a few scarce dishes, a television, and mosquito nets dangling from various places. The smell of burning trash filled the air accompanied by the sound of other houses' stereos and TVs, as loud as if you were in the very room they were coming from. Extension cords were the source of electricity and lights dangled from the rafters in the ceiling. Yes, rafters. The roof was made of tin metal; it more closely resembled a decaying barn, only the cows lived under the house. I'm not sure why they even had cows; they were too skinny to really be able to feed much of anyone.

This was just a mere moment in my life, yet this is their reality, this is how they live. . .

This was a description of a house that hosted our cell group in the Northern part of Thailand. It was something that I sat down to write about and the Lord seemed pulled it out of me. I sat down prepared to listen and in just a brief moment, I felt so strongly the need to write this down. As I look back over this, I can smell the neighboring scents all stewing together of an odor I find hard to describe. My nostrils tickle a little when I remember the breeze that floated through the open gaps in the wall. Yet, we were together; we were sharing stories of how Jesus worked in our lives, sharing culture, and growing together. Before we met together, we shared food that had been prepared for us.

Oh I wish I could have been a little braver, but there were little fish swimming around in the soup, skeletons and eyeballs still attached; I did not want to offend this culture. Praise God that Randi's (one of the team) stomach was stronger than mine could ever be. I still take the stance that fish are our friends and not food, best depicted by the wonderful movie (*Finding Nemo.*) Don't get me wrong, I was fed that evening, blessedly so, but I just could not get one of those fish into my mouth.

Sitting beside someone that doesn't speak your language, doesn't know your name, and lives somewhere so very different from where you are, but at the same time having so much in common because of the One who created you; there is something so remarkable about that. You share a faith that runs deeper than earth itself, one in Christ. I can't begin to describe to you how it was to listen to these people share their stories (with Brandon as our translator) and even before him translating, knowing that it was going to bring you closer to each other.

There is something so powerful in hearing someone else's story of anyone that has overcome something. It makes all the past struggles and future struggles a little more bearable. We all struggle in our life. We all go through things when we are not sure how or where we stand in, but hearing stories of how God has redeemed these monsters of events is the most beautiful thing I have ever witnessed.

Rice

I am not a rice farmer which maybe explains why I am bad at it! First of all, this is by far the most time consuming, back-laborious thing that I can ever imagine. To plant and harvest rice, first the soil must be prepared. This is done by a machine you walk behind that is very heavy and I am glad it was not my duty. The rice is planted in large quantities. Once is has arrived at a certain needed growth, it is uprooted, the field is flooded, and the rice must be separated and replanted in order to grow. Sounds simple enough, but I want you to imagine the hottest day your body has ever recalled.

The sun is beating down on you, and you are sweating out pours you never knew existed, not to mention the odor that comes with it, yes, I promise, these are the conditions they work in.

Now after you have uprooted the old rice buddies, (as I call them) you have to put them into bundles. Once you have prepared the field, it's time to set to work. Get ready to pull up your pants and take off your shoes because you are about to step into mud. Not just any mud mind you, but mud that has fertilizer, bugs, and an aroma so strong, you don't want to ask what it is coming from.

There are pinchy bugs that can latch on to your feet, snakes, and other random things also lurking in this foot and a half of watery mush. Now bend over half way, and prepare to have this be your stance for the next several days, from sunrise to sunset. The plant has to be just the right distance away from the other ones, not too close and not too far away. To plant these, you must separate them from the pack and gently but firmly push it into the ground, covering your hand with sludge. It needs to go in at least as deep as your thumb, if not a little further.

It startles me as I think of this in my current life situation. It seems sometimes as believers in the faith of Christ as Savior, we are often "planted" with other "like" people. We grow very well, and we think we are doing great! However, much like this rice, if it is not uprooted and spread out, it would choke off the other plants and have very little chance for survival. It is then replanted into the same field, but with room enough to grow. I am not saying we aren't able to stay close as friends, not at all. What I am saying is that we can't always thrive on the same patch of soil. We can still be involved in the same activities; we just can't completely rely on each other to the same degree.

It is good to have fellow believers to share life with! We can still have close relationships and help each other out, but sometimes in order to grow, we need to be uprooted and replanted and to be able to cling to the promises ourselves. That is why the plants are planted close together; they still need each other. However, our lifeline is cut when we no longer can be supported by anyone else around us, just the soil, and that soil is Jesus. He has equipped us with everything we need and some days, I find myself feeling like I'd like to be in that congested rice patch, before it is uprooted and replanted.

When I feel like I am being uprooted, sometimes I struggle with feeling like I have lost my roots, and I will never be replanted. It is something I believe I will struggle with for a long time. Sometimes the uprooting isn't a life uproot, it's just something that needs a little work; not a major relocation or a horror in my life. It seems He wants to keep transplanting us so we can grow, and grow well. He wants to get rid of the bad stuff that is keeping us from growing, and ultimately, things that are keeping us from Him. I am not saying separate yourself from the body of believers.

I am simply saying that you still need to be close and fellowship, just not clinging to each other and suffocating. Nor am I saying he is taking himself from you or you from Himself. He is the soil and the caretaker. It's a beautiful mystery, and again, an imperfect analogy. Know that we need each other and we get to bless each other. It also encourages me to know that feeling like I've been pried from the very dirt I stand on to know that God often has a plan and a purpose in it.

I will never forget that day in the rice field. I can honestly say I had a great time even though I wasn't able to last as long as everyone else. I can NOT imagine this being my every day job. More than a week of 12 hour days for them is equivalent to working only an hour for minimum wage in the US. For me, this was a new experience; of course it would be a thrilling event. I am grateful that

I was able to volunteer some time, so that they could reap a larger harvest without having to endure so much back pain. I now have a MUCH larger appreciation every time I see a bag of rice. I KNOW how much work that was. I do my best to say a prayer to bless those that planted it. Maybe someday soon, (or maybe we already have), you or I will have eaten rice that I have planted.

CHAPTER 12

A small room with some windows, bright yellowish-green colored walls, a chair, simple lighting, and a heater for winter. I knew this place yet somehow, I was off in my projected location…again. I saw this room dedicated as a prayer room. It was nothing fancy, just a place that was secluded and alone, a place to seek refuge with the Lord, a place to draw near to him and a place to dance. I saw this place in a vision while I was praying what God had next for me after Thailand, but I'll come back to this in a little bit later. I just wanted to get your mind thinking and imagining of such a wonderful place that is a "come as you are, no frills, just God and you" sort of place. Yes. Are you thinking of it? Perfect. Now I'll move on.

God shakes my expectations almost daily. Sometimes I get shaken so hard that I wonder if I heard him correctly in the first place. It seems sometimes He uses my idea of what He's shown to get me to a place and the throw me for a complete loop once I am there.

While we were in northern Thailand, we spent a great deal of time with the children. I loved these wonderful little lives. I still think of their smiling faces as we spent the days playing games with them, teaching them our "new" American games. I got to practice my Thai a little bit while calling out the numbers for a made-up version of Steal the Bacon. They were simple games, but it was so much fun.

These priceless children stole my heart…but the woman I mentioned earlier stole my heart a little more. She shared with me her story and let me live life with her for a few days. She was a blessing to talk to and I miss her dearly as I think of it all right now. It's so difficult to know exactly how to share with you all the remarkable things this woman and her husband have done together. I am truly blessed to know that this woman is serving her guts out to the amazing Savior.

Father. Let me use these words as an offering to you, please put them in the order you would like them to come out, and would it be your art coming through. Help me write the real story and not what people just want to hear. How can I most glorify you in this story that you are writing?

The name of the woman that happened to steal my heart is Hannah. Hannah is young, around the same age I am and I haven't arrived at 30 yet. She might be a few years older or younger than me, I can't remember, but I know she is strong. Her faith is magnificent. This woman Hannah lives with her husband and they run this wonderful place where they house the abandoned and homeless children while raising her own children. She and her husband provide for these children by working extremely hard and trusting God to bring them the finances. They rely on the support of others around the world to feed themselves.

One of the most heart-felt stories Hannah shared with me while I was there with them is the story of how her child Manna was born. While Hannah was quite far along in her pregnancy with her daughter, she needed to get supplies for the home, so she jumped on the moped that they use and rely on for most of their transportation (unless they are taking all of the children somewhere). While she was driving, a larger vehicle didn't see her, forced her off the road, and she was involved in an accident. The doctors didn't give her much hope about her child surviving such an ordeal; Hannah was in bad shape herself. It is the power of prayer that makes this story so amazing. Not only was Hannah ok, but so was the baby when she delivered. I got the privilege to hold Manna, now a healthy toddler and a true blessing from heaven.

I felt extraordinarily drawn to Hannah and the other woman that helped things be made possible. The children were drawn to Brandon and the others and the three of us would sit down with the younger children and chat. They were gracious in being patient with me while we worked through our language barrier.

Universal Language

That evening we were watching a special program on their television set. I am not sure how they got this channel or if it was an American DVD, but the speaker was from a well known band from the United States and I found myself drawn to the program. I don't think it was simply because it was the only program in English I had heard since we arrived in Thailand, but because I believe God was drawing me to what he had to say through this speaker.

The man was talking about the universal language and how it should be love. Love is something we all should be able to relate to, and draw closer from, but I fear too many people have been hurt and their hearts are broken from lack of love, or tainted love. What this man said was that it was pain. I won't copy his words, because I would then be plagiarizing, but I can give you my take on the subject. As I sat there listening to this man's message, I felt my heart becoming really tight; I knew he was right.

Everyone knows pain. We have taken chances only to come back feeling void and empty or have being beaten. I reflected over my time already in Thailand to see the most desperate of poverty scattered all around me, people desperate to make it just one more day. I went to hospitals where you leave your shoes at the door and the doctors don't have the tools to be able to help their patients, the hurt in the faces of their loved ones realizing they won't be around much longer. I see in the states, people being betrayed and stabbed in the back for self-advancement. It doesn't matter how big or small, everyone knows pain.

I felt my throat becoming closed as I choked up trying to keep myself and my emotions in control, since I was the only one paying close attention to the detail of the program. I began to think about Jesus and how he knows so much about pain, both physical and emotional. This man was God, and he came to life to live among his people, and came to bring a message of hope, salvation, and eternal freedom only to be rejected. If the rejection wasn't enough pain, he then was betrayed and abandoned by the ones that should have been standing beside him. Then the worst imaginable physical pain occurred as he endured the beatings for things he did not do; his punishment for a crime he did not commit. He then had to watch his people ignore the freedom that he gave in dying on the cross; I am sure his heart hurts still.

Jesus knows about pain very well. He knows how each one of us feels at our most desperate of hours, he knows our weakness and our sorrows. It doesn't end there though; there is a promise of hope. Jesus endured all of those things to show his great love for us, his children. He came to show us the way to heaven, HIM. He came to teach us about love, and show us how much he loves us.

Someday, I hope the message of love is louder than the message of pain and that across the nations, the one that speaks louder will be love. There are amazing things happening with love being spread across the nations, and those stories bring me hope, I know that God is bigger than all the pain in the world, and his message, his truth, is the one that stands throughout all generations.

Elephants

On our last day in the north, we took the children to an elephant show and elephant rides. On our ride there in the back of sungtows, it was so evident of how Jesus had been working in these children's lives. Even though there was a massive language barrier still, they were singing radiantly about Jesus, in their language. They were excited to share their English with us, and laughed when we tried to share our Thai with them.

The elephant show was fantastic. They called on one of the leaders, Brandon, to be part of the show and he had an elephant step on his backside. It was pretty neat to see someone each one of the children from the home could relate to up there, as Brandon has visited them several times. Elephants are extremely large creatures and they fascinate me beyond all measure. I love life, and this is a life we only get to see in a zoo or circus here in the states, but several times when we were up north, people would be riding elephants normal as can be. (My first elephant sighting was a blessed one that was followed by my shouting Chaang, (the Thai word for elephant) but that had been several weeks earlier.)

It then came time to ride the elephants. Each adult went with two of the children. I had the most wonderfully happy two young girls; they were so excited to have this chance to go on the elephant.

There were these cool saddles that were lifted off of the elephants back; it was so much more exciting than riding horses ever could be. The movement of an elephant is extremely graceful, but dramatic when you are sitting on one. Imagine slow fluid movements of great capacity as you sway in a large circle as they walk. I loved it! It brought me back to the days of my youth going on horseback riding trails, only on a larger scheme of course. I am privileged to have been able to participate in this event, as well as being able to provide the funds to let these children take part in something so special.

While we were there having a blast with the children, one adult female from our group grabbed my hand and started crying. She clung to my hand and then began pouring out her young heart to me. She was 23 years old at the time with two young children and a full heart that needed to be released. She begged me to consider coming back, and to this day, I am still trying to find a way to go back and spend some more time with her. I had no idea that I was able to make such an impact on someone in such a few small days. It amazes me the way God ordains and works out friendships in his special way. Time means nothing to him and he can create a friendship in an instant if he wants; that is exactly what happened with this woman.

I spent the ride home talking with the adult women who resided there. . The others played and kept the children entertained. It felt a little odd to me that God had me spending the majority of my time focused on the adults, seeing as we came to an orphanage and all, but I proceeded on.

His workers need encouragement. We are all in this crazy world as a mission field (and a true battlefield against Satan) and do we ever need people to come and run alongside of us. I don't imagine this to be like cheerleaders who stand on the side lines of a football game, but instead as people that come along side of you in this marathon of life that run a portion of life with you. We all need to take turns taking the baton and running alongside of each other. Encouragement goes a long way. This was and is especially true for these adult workers that are still people and still need love and care as they spend themselves caring and nurturing these special children. They are doing a wonderful job, and God supplies them with love, but it was and is an honor to have been able to share in their lives as well.

I think this was one of the coolest realizations of the whole trip; in the three weeks that I was in Thailand, I was being able to bring encouragement to those that were already there. It was great to be able to go to where the people were working and serving in some difficult environments and be able to work beside them and just give them a break, some sort of relief and show them that they are still valuable. How often, when we are in the middle of a big project or sometime, when we can get so caught up on serving and taking care of others, do we forget our importance. Not that it needs to be our focus, but everyone is so important to God and very special. It was such a privilege to be able to bless those that spend so much time working with the people and that concentrate so much on blessing others. It was like giving fuel to a fire, to revive and stir up and spur one another on for those that are living there and staying there.

I reflected over the course of our trip how a lot of our ministry was doing that. We went along with the people who are there doing very amazing but difficult things. We spent time in the slums with the people, shared our hearts with them, and loved them. We also loved them with the people that spend all their time with them. We went to the orphanages and spent time with the leaders who are there and some time individually with children, learned their love and passions, and were able to continue with them. We did fun things with other people who have been there a long time to remind them that they are not doing things in vain, that they are making a lasting impact. Even in the three weeks' time there, I saw how God put and used our time there in a creative puzzle of perfection.

Lasting effects

While I don't know all the effects of our time in Thailand, I can tell you how it affected me and the things I do know and how God taught me. It was such a simple trip, full of adventures, but the truth of God was shared through the nation of Thailand. It was a chance to go to the ends of the earth... I believe that is anywhere that takes you out of your comfort zone... and Thailand certainly did that.

I can, however, tell you about Tukta. When we were in Thailand, (I don't know how long before we arrived in Thailand) Tukta hung around with the people we were hanging around with. I can tell you also that when we arrived she was very much a Buddhist. Her faith was based on the surroundings of her family's belief system. Throughout our time in Thailand we got to share our lives with her, our experience with God and each one of us were blessed in getting to know her much better. In three weeks I can say that Tukta is a friend that I have kept in touch with, and I am so very blessed to have her in my life.

She came with us to the north when we went to the children's home and when we shared stories about the Lord; who He is and what He has done. There was one day before we went north that I was walking around the road and found her and her friend. I was reading my bible and watching the boys play basketball and decided to read the entire book of Matthew out loud. I could see her amazement and saw God beginning to work in her. She asked questions, and I should have asked her if she just wanted to practice her English or if she was interested, but I didn't think it mattered.

When we left Thailand, Tukta was still a Buddhist, but it seemed she was more open to the idea that Jesus might be the truth after all. Our time with Tukta was over, but our hearts were still with her. I know Tukta is one that I pray for quite often. Our time with Tukta was part of the puzzle that brought her to know the Lord. I don't know all the steps of it all, but in keeping in touch with her, and meeting some of the people that came after us that lived life with and shared Christ with her, I can say, that Tukta is now not only following Jesus, but she is doing a missionary training school and is a cofounder of a woman's ministry that helps women of poverty become empowered to make an honest income by recycling plastic bags and making them into purses, bags and other items. I am honored to know the other cofounder from my life in Michigan, and am so proud of her as well for following her dream and the call of God to do what seemed impossible, as well as watching God do the impossible through them both. If you are interested in the ministry that I am talking about you can check it out at www.thaisongfairtrade.org.

CHAPTER 13

Today I was sitting in my room wondering about passion and thinking back on my time spent in Thailand. I had written in my journal that my life would be completely ruined for the ordinary, and it truly has been since I have returned. It seems like I go bumping around, trying to find my way, to make some sort of normalcy out of my circumstances or situations. I find myself all tangled up in lots of difficult challenges. As I looked through my journal, my thoughts and words seemed to dance on the page. I came alive when I was there in Thailand; it was amazing.

This chapter is extremely difficult for me to write. It is one of the last about Thailand. There is so much about those simple three weeks that changed my life forever. It feels like I am saying goodbye to a piece of my heart when I finish writing about this. I have spent a lot of time pouring my memories and thoughts, reliving all the awesome things God did and has done through this trip. It feels like a piece of closure that I have been prolonging. While I know that the sooner I finish writing this book, the sooner you will get to read it, it is still difficult. I have put literally years into the creation of this book but it is time to move forward and beyond these words of Thailand. God has more to do; He's not done yet.

The final days

Our last days in Thailand were full trying to fit everything into the last few moments that we had left. Being halfway around the world, none of us were certain if the Lord would ever take us back to this place again. We played games with the group at BJD, the place I referred to in the beginning of this story, with the students and another American team that was there the same time we were. It was evident then the bond that we all had formed.

The next day was the hardest day of the trip for me. We went to the slums to say goodbye to all of our friends that we had met while we were there. My heart was especially hurting for a woman named Yai Noy. I mentioned her earlier in this story, and I find this is the right time to reintroduce her. Yai Noy had lost her husband a few years ago, and now is alone in the slums. She is quite elderly, I am not entirely sure how old though.

She is sassy, but wonderful and full of spunk. I miss this woman to this day as I think about her, of her life and the things that God has done. I still remember the day I spent with Yai Noy, working together to sort through her clothes, helping her say goodbye to some things that she didn't need to hold onto. This particular day in the slums was not too different, only a bit more emotional than the others. It was also the day we were celebrating with a worship party at BJD so we were bringing some people back with us. It would double as a farewell party for those that were leaving.

We brought Yai Noy with us to go and get Thai massages. It was weird for me to go and spend this time pampering myself, but being able to partake in it with Yai Noy was incredible. We had to split up the group so I went with one of my friends to a different place. Even though Yai Noy had lived in Thailand her entire life, she had never gotten to experience a Thai massage. Being able to bless this woman, to allow her to experience something so rich in her culture, and letting her feel like a princess was well worth the awkwardness. She had spent so many days struggling and just trying to make it. I love this woman, and I pray with all of my heart that I will get to meet her again this side of heaven.

Later that evening when we were at the party, it was blissful to be able to worship the Lord of Heaven with people that can't speak the same language. They had the words in both in English and Thai so we sang the language that we knew how to speak. It was the most beautiful thing I have ever been part of in my entire life. The Holy Spirit was moving freely in the room, setting hearts free and bringing hope. To be able to be a part of such fresh and pure worship without the politics or concerns was spectacular.

We danced our hearts out! I enjoyed dancing with another woman from the slums. She grabbed my arm and we flung our bodies rhythmically around the room with several others. I hadn't laughed or felt the love of the Lord like that in such a long time. It was freeing. It was so refreshing and powerful to be in the presence of so many people that love Jesus so deeply and were singing their guts out to praise Him.

On this trip, and many times in my life, I have found myself trying to negotiate with God. It sometimes feels like I have a better way to do it. That night at the party was no different than the night in Pattaya when I felt like I was supposed to share the song that God had allowed me to write. I told him I thought it wasn't the right time, but there was still that urging from him that I was to play this song. I didn't do it in Pattaya but it seemed I got another chance. I asked Brandon if I could play a song I wrote since I felt the Lord's urging to give me a second chance.

I'd like to say it went well, but it was awful. I wish I would have obeyed in the first place. I was bumpy and played terribly. I think my lesson was one of obeying; I am still working on not trying to negotiate with God. His plan will always work out better than my plan, even if it isn't better for me. He works all things out for HIS good. That doesn't mean things won't be bumpy and painfully hard, but it does mean that we should still listen to, obey, and follow him. I still did what I needed to do and felt better for obeying. I am not even sure why God had me share my song. Did my horrible guitar playing skills benefit anyone else? Maybe it was just to bring me more humility.

That night my new Thai friend gave me a tiara. When we were in Pattaya, he found out that my pastor in Michigan called me princess, so he thought it was fitting to give me a tiara. I find it most refreshing that I spent most of this trip trying to bless others, yet the blessings seemed to be heaped and multiplied back to me in bulk. I truly felt like a princess of the Highest King of all kings dancing and singing with my tiara; that token and gesture meant a lot. God allowed me not to rip someone off out of giving a blessing. I love to bless people and I don't always do well at receiving them.

Saying Goodbye

On our last full day in Thailand, we went to the aquarium we had tried to go to the first day of our adventure. It was crazy to think our entire trip had gone by, that we had made such close friends that began right there at Ocean World. We got to spend it with our friend Nida whom we had gotten closer with over our time in Thailand. She did a remarkable job throughout the trip showing us places and I have really enjoyed being her friend. I have some wonderful pictures of the two of us as well as the other girls on the trip too. It was a nice way to spend the last day of the trip, debriefing and getting ready to go home. I was not ready.

We got back to BJD really late and we still had packing to do. I knew that I would not be sleeping. I had a little bit of "goodbye anxiety." I did not want to miss telling one person goodbye. It hurt too much leaving; not being able to at least hug these knew treasured friends. Luckily, I was able to do so. . My eyes were full of tears that I tried to choke back, but I did not do a good job.

Our night of packing was filled with laughter and memories and a little bit of an annoyance. When I developed some pictures of when I was in Pattaya, my memory chip got a virus. When collecting all the pictures on Brett's computer, the virus ended up taking over that. Needless to say, a lot of time was spent cleaning it off. Despite this little snafu, it was still so good to be able to be goofy with Fon and Tukta one last night.

Before the sun raised, Kim, the other American team, and myself were packed and ready to get on the sungtow to go to the airport. Several of our friends rode along with us. I have never been part of a more sobering experience. The Thai are generally not emotional people; they don't show their emotion. I on the other hand am almost the opposite. I am a very passionate person that comes out in emotions that I sometimes keep captive. That morning there wasn't anything that I could do from holding back my tears. I was heartbroken to be leaving my new friends. We sang, we laughed, and we cried on that trip to the airport. At the doors, we hugged and cried some more. Then, Kim and I entered into our final part of the journey, the journey home.

Turbulence

Kim and I were not seated together on our flight to Chicago. She and Randi had flown out from Green Bay while I had flown out of Minneapolis. We met up in Chicago, so that was where our journey would end. From Thailand to Tokyo, we were seated together and the trip went much faster than I could have ever imagined. I spent the time writing in my journal and reflecting over the trip.

The flight from Tokyo to Chicago was a much rougher ride for me. I was seated in the middle of the mid-section of seats surrounded by two men that I did not know. Kim was several rows in front of me. By this time, I had been awake for way too many hours. I finally fell asleep and had a dream about Tukta and Tee who had come with us to Maha Sarakaham. I recall in the dream being on a bumpy bus going somewhere still in Thailand, and something was not right.

As I slept, the plane experienced several amounts of turbulence that I must have incorporated into my dream. I awoke with quite a start, my arms flying in all directions trying to "get away" from whatever in my dream was holding me tight. I am not sure, but it felt like a force of loneliness and like I was being torn from my existence. In doing so, I am pretty sure the two men next to me were hit.

I felt bad for those men and the rest of the people around me who had been victim to my flailing arms and lack of sleep. When I snapped to, it was the most somber feeling. I knew that once we arrived at our destination, we would not be with our Thailand friends; we would be back in the states. The reality of it all really hit me; I knew the journey home would be long.

I looked around the plane at the faces of those surrounding me, in the distant and closer rows. I was trying not to be stalker-like, but I just couldn't help but notice my surroundings. I saw a deep beauty that resides to the depths of my being. I saw God's craftsmanship and love just being lavished on them. Humans are truly a masterpiece, to be able to think and write and cry and laugh. Seeing all these masterpieces on my flight back to the states helped my mind just reflect on God's holiness. So many lives, so many pieces of art; humans are truly miracles.

When we arrived back in Chicago, I discovered my turbulence hadn't finished. We arrived later than expected; I missed the flight and then my second flight which they rescheduled me on had been canceled. Kim and I looked at each other and weren't quite sure of how things would go, but since I had more time, I walked with her to her gate and said goodbye. This was the time I wished I had packed more things in my carry-on bag. I didn't think on the ride home that I would need to pack as many things as I did on the way there. I was wrong.

Three hours, later Kim called to ask how my flight home was, and I told her Chicago still looked lovely. It had been several hours and there were no sights of a flight home for me. Exhausted, I was bumped from three more flights and had another flight canceled. I wished I had been able to sleep more on the flight to Chicago. It had been 32 hours since leaving Thailand and I think I slept about 4 non-consecutive hours. At about 8PM that night, I found out that there would be no more flights going to Minneapolis for the rest of the evening. I went to the reservation desk to find a human and told them all my flights had been canceled. I was hoping to get a room somewhere near the airport. I needed to sleep but really, I just wanted to go home, or better yet, back to Thailand.

They checked my flight status and decided that I could get a room due to the circumstances of my flight being canceled, even though I had been in the airport 11 extra hours. I had a flight scheduled for 7:00am the next morning. I looked to see where they gave me a food voucher and hotel room for. The room would be at the Hilton, slightly different than my housing arrangements in Thailand. I didn't have a credit card, so I had some problems checking into the hotel. Finally, I was able to get settled into my room. What a drastic difference! I wasn't quite sure how to get settled back into the lifestyle here in America.

In the middle of the night, or 9pm (I was a bit jet-lagged to say the least), I received a phone call from a familiar number, but again, I was really out of it. I answered the phone and said good morning to a really confused friend asking if I was still in Chicago. At first I didn't even know where I was exactly but then remembered that yes, I was still residing in the windy city. After that phone call with my friend Alex, I had wonderful dreams and slept soundly until morning when it was time to head to the airport and make it through customs. Since I only had my carry-on bag, it wasn't so difficult getting on. I am glad I was able to shower before I headed back. I sent a text message to my friend who was coming to pick me up at the airport to let her know the new plans for the flight. Once I got to my gate, I found my flight had been delayed, again.

Three more delays past by before I finally was able to board the plane and return to Minneapolis. God did so many things to make our trip full circle. The day that I arrived back in Minneapolis was no different. I flew out of E10 and I returned through the gate E10. Having my feet back in Minnesota, I was just a few hours away from my home and my puppy. It was the weirdest feeling I can express to you. It felt surreal, like I had never left, but I knew my life had been changed forever.

CHAPTER 14

The first moments were a blur. The trip home was filled with nostalgia for a country I had grown to love, familiar, yet so very different. I thought I would miss my favorite kind of soda, the beloved Diet Mountain Dew, while I was gone. Right after I got back, I bought two 20 ounce bottles of it in the airport thinking it would be a great treat to welcome myself home. Boy was I wrong; the stuff that I once craved and longed for tasted bitter and like poison. It looked as though Thailand had cured my addiction to once tasty drink, in three short weeks. Even though I no longer craved my favorite soda, my heart was instantly lonely for the fellowship that had been happening in Thailand. I was grateful that a gracious friend to came to the airport to pick me up accompanied by great conversation that we had on the way home.

I was in Menomonie for about an hour once I arrived back from the airport. It was weird finally being there. I still longed for Thailand, but after being stuck in Chicago over night, it was nice to be home, even if it was only for an hour before I had to grab a few more items for a week of camp I would be working at. I rushed to my dad's house to see my puppy Wembley, I only would have a few hours to see him before I would leave him there again for a week. Wembley barked at me a good deal and told me off for leaving him but I saw how much fun he had while at my dad's and how much my aunt and dad loved him. Leaving him for another week was very difficult, but I knew that the Lord had this all arranged before I even left for Thailand.

I ended up spending too much time at my dad's and didn't have enough time to get my laundry done so everything I took with me to Thailand, I had to bring with me to camp. I am glad that I had stopped in Menomonie to collect a few more articles of clothing and some American supplies.

My first night at camp, a dream came to me. I was beyond tired when I went to bed that particular night I remember this dream vividly; I woke up with that same awe feeling that let me know it was from the Lord. There were some key points to this dream that spoke to me; in my dream I was in a new place, but it felt very familiar. There was this rectangular room with tables in it that was wider than long. It had a guitar with a cross behind it in the right front corner of the room, as well as a yellow-green walled place and a gray floored area with couches in it; my friend Steve was sitting on them. In my dream there was also a YYC airport code as well as the physical wall signs on the walls of the airport.

The first thing I did when I woke up was grab my computer to see if by some "random chance" I could get the internet. All my campers were still asleep so I was very quiet and kept my laptop underneath the blanket. I opened the internet with ease and was surprised that I found a wireless connection. I got into a website to check flight dates. I felt my fingers typing September 17, looked at my college schedule and realized I might be able to take a trip starting on a Thursday and coming back on a Tuesday, only missing one day of class. I put in the end date for a week later just to check on dates and pressed enter to see where this mystery trip was taking me: Calgary, Alberta Canada; interesting. I wondered if this was the same place that Steve would be leading a Discipleship training School there.

I checked a different date to see if that would work and how much the ticket would cost. However, for some reason it felt like screaming monkeys were jumping in my brain, telling me that was not the right date. It was just over a month and a half until the dates that I typed into the computer, the dates that I would maybe be leaving once again. I couldn't help but get a little excited at the possibility of another adventure. , but I didn't want to get my hopes up or read too far into anything, but there was something in this dream that wouldn't leave me alone. I gave it to the Lord and prayed that he would direct the days into place and if this trip were to happen, he'd make a way for it to come to pass.

The rest of the week that I spent at camp was filled with awesome adventures. It was filled with sharing the things Christ did over the trip and seeing lives being changed here in the states. It was difficult to be back, but I was uncomfortably comfortable.

The next several weeks were a beautiful mix of adventures, including another dream. I might need to remind you that I know not all of my dreams are from God however I do know there are some that are. This is another one of them that I knew was from Him. This dream was a song that was being written, the perfect blend between melody and harmony, between treble and bass; it was stunning. With the song being written, I saw the place in the other dream I had had previously and lot of things that were going to happen. He told me that I was to teach on encouragement, bring unity and be an example of reckless obedience. In this dream, Steve was there again. I knew I would be going to visit him. It really was the most spectacular thing; I have never had a dream in music like this before and I knew the song must have been symbolic of something. When I woke from this dream, the song remained with me. I knew that while I was awake, I was to pray a lot about this and wait for something to confirm this place.

I was supposed to go to a wedding in Minnesota, but because I couldn't find a dog watcher, I didn't end up getting to go. However, I did get an invitation (only from another invite) to this go and listen to this special speaker talking about following dreams. (This also included everything that had happened inside of me throughout the trip to Thailand). It was the most refreshing and encouraging message I had heard in a long time. God instills dreams inside our heart, and he allows us to chase them while at the same time, chasing him. He designs us to be followers of him, and he has big dreams for his people and for sharing his message of life and salvation.

While on my trip to Thailand, I was talking to a friend the conversation went to dreams. These dreams are not necessarily the kind that happen when your eyes are shut and you are asleep, but the dreams that control your passions, or the passions that control your dreams.

We talked about how so many people have forgotten to dream, or they have dreams within the confines of something known; even if it seems big, it is limited. It seems that we have let life come to control us. We settle ourselves into debt or the desires to have more things or have what we think we need and we forget to dream. Is having a "something" a dream? Well, I suppose it could be considered one. We as a society have lived in this weird place where life seems to come and go without being noticed, either that, or we are so desperate to be noticed that we go to extremes to stand out.

All in all, what is the driving force? What is the passion?

Over the past few years, I have seen a few people that have gained that sense of dreaming, where nothing is impossible in the love of the Lord (and if it is in the Lord's will, all things are possible).

That night was a great and perplexing confirmation of how the Lord works and makes things even more real. I had started writing a blog the night prior to going to hear this speaker and I felt that the Lord was telling me to take a break and a pause and wait to finish writing. The next day, I went to listen to this wonderful women speak and share some things with us... and it was exactly about dreams, again, not the kind that you have when you are sleeping... but the ones that give us passion and reason. It truly was really incredible and allowed me to go deeper in the post I was writing.

I began to think again of why our dreams go so unrecognized, or when we push them far aside when really, they may have been the beginning of a blessing the Lord wanted to bestow upon us in our lives. I think of high school, of how the dream of who we become is more on the sustainment and trying to be popular or accepted when Jesus already said that He accepts us. That is all that really matters.

With that, I'm wondering, what is your dream? What is it that you have thought about once or twice, maybe have thought it was too big or beyond your reach and then as a result, gave it up thinking it ridiculous? What were you doing along the journey that caused this dream to get tucked away and out of site?

Was it money? Or was it the chasing of money, perhaps? Was it an idea that you needed a large amount of money not even in a greed sort of way? Could it be chasing the "need" faded the dream?

Was it the words of someone else? Was it simply the need to survive? Was it self-doubt?

Or did the dream just kind of get put away with the toil of everyday life . . .

Have you had a taste of your dream? Is it just right there in front of you? Is it hard? Has it been ripped from your hands, stomped on, discarded and left you broken? Just think about this for a moment.

And if you don't have a dream, I encourage you to take time and find a way to have one. Don't keep putting it away. We can financially survive and still have a dream. I am not saying go into a zillion dollar debt, but seek the Lord and let Him instill those dreams . . . and don't be afraid.

Looking back over my life, with the struggles and burdens, and the joys and trials and blissful moments, I can see how some things were just a stepping stone to let the Lord teach me and allow me to grow. Some things He wants me just to see, and begin to dream IN HIM again. . . and some things I still have no idea the meaning behind, why I was allowed to experience the moments, the pains or the gains. Sometimes holding onto those dreams can be the most difficult struggle you can face. Knowing when it's time to let go of a dream or do the exact opposite and chase one that God has given you can be very hard. I believe God allows us to dream to keep us alive, to keep us passionate and to keep us focused on him.

That night was another God-arranged occurrence, one I didn't know then, was a stepping stone to following a dream God gave me. My friend Steve was in China, and I knew that the chances of him getting online were next to none while he was there. China is a closed country that doesn't allow people in to do ministry, so what you talk about and read online is very much a dance of words. With this being said I was on my social network and my computer gave me notice that Steve was online and had accepted my friend request. This is the first time I could look at his profile to see what his networks were for, to see where in Canada he would be.

I began a conversation with him and asked how things were going in China. I then began to ask questions about where he would be joining the staff at the school he was talking about. I told him about my dreams with the airport code and the music, leaving some details aside (so I could let God work those out). In our conversation, I began looking at the website for the school he was teaching at. Amazingly, the airport was the one I would need to fly into in order to visit.

While he was talking about praying for the students that were coming, (they were still praying for more applications to come in), and I felt a twinge in my heart that I needed to apply for this training school. I didn't know where the outreach destinations were going, but I was suddenly overwhelmed at the possibility that this might be were God wanted me to go. I arranged with him that I would be coming to visit Canada, and for the first time since he was in China, I knew where he would be at. I love that God organized the details before I knew. There was no way that I could have planned this and detailed it as neatly as God did. There was no way I could have picked the airport code to an airport I had never heard of. No way. That was beside God.

I didn't tell Steve about the urges in my heart to apply for the school. I was already enrolled in another semester of college, signed into a lease, and had no idea how to work out the financial aid out since I had already accepted the amount and loans were already taken out. While having these twinges in my heart to apply, I wasn't scared that I wouldn't get accepted, but that I WOULD. I asked God how I would pay for this trip, and I heard him say the social network that I was part of. I didn't understand what he meant entirely, but I looked at the cost of the school and the cost of outreach. I then divided that by the amount of friends I had on the network, and amazingly, if each friend contributed just 10 dollars, I'd have more than enough. I pushed the thoughts aside and asked God that he would again, arrange it if it needed to be.

My mind was filled with possibilities and my heart was full of prayers. My days were filled with prayer, reading the bible and seeking God's will for this possibility. One of my solace times was reading Proverbs 3:5 6: Trust in The Lord with all your heart, and lean not on your own understandings, but in all your ways acknowledge Him and He will make your path straight.

I know so many of us have heard this verse, and probably many have memorized it, but during this time it was such a refreshing and confirming voice that I didn't have to seek out or try to figure out the entire puzzle. The next segment is an excerpt from my blog so you get the idea of the process, because I am also certain that the process speaks more than the outcome. It is mindboggling to look back at this and see how God worked the timing out.

Tonight has been such a crazy night, but crazy in a good way, and wanting to soak in the presence of the LORD. Just to be so saturated in Him. It is really amazing how God places His purposes on different people's hearts. I guess I can't really mention more about this yet, because timing is crucial.

But just again, in timing, it requires trusting. What does our entire heart look like, is there a fraction of doubt in our hearts, and is there contempt? How do we begin to trust with all of our hearts . .

The next part is a kicker too... and lean not on your own understandings. Over and over God has been showing me that I can't rely on just my understanding of something, but that if I give him complete control and trust Him with no attachments, He's got it under control. If he called Peter to walk out on the water and he didn't sink until he tried to trust in what he understood, then I wonder how many things I try to wrap my own understandings around.

I realize I am guilty this. Leaning on my own understandings, and even though I do some pretty crazy things, I find I often try to negotiate with God because I don't' get what he has asked me to do. I don't understand how His purpose looks, and this has been something I have been praying for over the last month.

In all your ways acknowledge Him, and he will make your path straight.

All.

I love the Lord These two verses that we have looked at over time so many times, that I have been blessed by before, just how much they really say, and how much of a blessing to live by they really can be. They are something quite simple and yet so complex.

CHAPTER 15

To the Ends of the Earth . . .

A song and verse had been dancing in my heart and mind; one so similar to this journey of trying to find what God's path was for me in the next few months (although it was more like months and months and months). This song and verse had been almost plaguing me; I kept wondering if God was speaking something special through them.

The verses: Matthew 28:18: Then Jesus came to them and said, "All authority in heaven and on earth has been given to me. 19 Therefore go and make disciples of all nations, baptizing them in the name of the Father and of the Son and of the Holy Spirit, 20 and teaching them to obey everything I have commanded you. And surely I am with you always, to the very end of the age."

The song which says: Jesus, I believe in you, and I will go, to the ends of the earth, the ends of the earth, for you alone are the Son of God and all the world will see, that you are God . . . (*Hillsong United.)*

For the longest time, I thought God wanted me to stay in America. There is a huge need for help and aid in this country and a lot of good that could be done. However, even before going to Thailand, I could feel my heart being tugged. I also remember talking to some people while I was in Thailand, being so convinced that America was where I was supposed to be. I love how God totally breaks me and changes things that I hold onto. He showed me that yes! there is a need here in America, but that doesn't mean that that is what I will forever be doing and it doesn't mean that I won't at some point be in America. I might also be LEAVING America.

I just know that the passions that were instilled in me a long time ago have gotten stronger and have also been expanded; the vision is a lot clearer now. Even though the location has broadened the concept is still the same. God has a plan for the Nations, including the one I am in, no matter which one it is. He may at any time request any of us to go to a different one. He knows where He wants us, and where the greatest purpose is in our being right where He puts us. Being willing to go, stay or wait is a beautiful challenge.

Everyone's calling and purpose is a great and unique thing. No one is more important than another. Jesus calls us to follow Him. He takes us to different places than each other, so it is important that we do not compare ourselves with one another. Our first priority is on following HIM. The last chapter of John describes this perfectly when Jesus had returned and he was talking to Peter and three times Jesus asks if Peter loves Him. Each time Peter answered yes, more saddened at each time that the Lord would have to ask three times that he loves Him. Jesus then tells him a bit of how his (Peter's) life/death would glorify Christ. Peter then asked about John and his life, and Jesus basically said it wasn't his business to wonder about him, Peter's was called to FOLLOW Him. It just goes to show that Jesus is concerned with our following of HIM. We need not get so caught up in others, but in following Him. We share Him with those we come in contact with, doing so with our words, and our love. Because of this is it a glorious thing when people are doing what they were created to do. If we are following Him, and we are ready to do as God requests, we will be fellowshipping with others, but focused on Christ. It really does become one on one with Jesus.

I know that I still have a lot more to learn in this very area of following. I can get frustrated if I seem to being asked to do all of the really difficult things that make me look somewhat foolish when it doesn't seem to matter if someone else is not. For me to follow Jesus, I have to know Him, and love Him. I just want to BE with HIM and following closely after Him. This was true for following God to Thailand, and it is still entirely true today when I type and try to retell you the story of how I bravely followed God and his purpose.(even if it didn't feel too brave.)

With this being said, I must continue to ask myself, am I really truly willing to go to the ends of the earth and make disciples of all nations? I asked myself this very question when I was in Thailand. You may ask, "Weren't you already on the other side of the world? Doesn't that classify as going to the ends of the earth?" You may be right on that note, but this for me is not just a one-time deal. I have found that the more I spend time with Jesus, the more I know that I am willing, even if I drag my feet a little bit, I am willing to do this. I know he's put this sense of urgency in my heart and has stirred up this passion because I am peacefully restless. I would love to bring the exciting things that are happening around the world back to America, the infectious fire that seems to have taken over. It is amazing. It is simply beautiful.

Not sure what to do, I made my decision I would go to Canada for 6 days, come back and finish my year of school in

Wisconsin, and then apply to and attend the school in Canada the following year. This way, I would have time to prepare the money and arrange a place for Wembley, and take care of my other responsibilities. I had prayed long and hard and even though my heart felt a little sad, I thought it would be the best decision I could make considering I had already signed a lease. After I registered for the semester of college in Wisconsin and was all set to spend that week in Canada, I really began to question if this was what I was supposed to do. As the dates that I originally looked at camp loomed in the distance, my own fear became relevant. What was the purpose of this trip? Was this really what God wanted? I didn't NEED to go to Canada, did I? If I were going next year, did I really need to go now?

When each thought of doubt came up, I took it to the Lord and asked him to confirm or deny if I was to go. I was desperate to have direction, to know if I was doing what HE wanted me to do, not what I wanted to do. I hesitated only a little too long and missed the first couple of dates that I was to fly out, (which would have been the first week of the school.) This school was a Discipleship Training School with Youth With A Mission (YWAM). The first 3 months are lecture phase that no two are the same. It is a time dedicated to learn more and embrace WHO God is, rather than just what He does. After the lecture phase is a cross-cultural outreach phase that allows what is taught to be put into practice. Steve would be a leader at this school and he came online and we had a good chat. He asked about my trip to Canada and through the online conversation and much prayer, I went ahead and did it. I bought my round trip, six day round-trip ticket.

The next two weeks of preparation for this trip were filled with odd closures. This college semester was purely miserable for me. I was so tired of hearing about the political side of things and my heart was far from my studies. I did try to put my entire effort into my classes, but there was something so distant from the class work and my heart. There was so much needless drama and people getting upset over such little things. Compared to my summer of a new way of life, this really troubled my heart. I made a promise to myself to try to love more deeply, live more freely, and follow Jesus no matter how the drama felt. I wish that I always was able to hold this mentality; it is still a struggle for me when I see things falling apart, but it still is my intention to live above drama. I have not fully achieved this, but it is a goal for my life.

I began to get really excited for the possibilities in Canada. For the six days I would be there, so much could happen! I was really excited to see how the dreams that I had fit into the whole part of me being there. It seemed like God had personally set up meetings to be divinely approached. For instance, I needed to have a walk with a friend and a conversation of closure before leaving for Canada. I thought it might have had to wait a week while I was gone, and I was wrong. When I was least expecting it to, this person showed up on my doorstep and we took a walk around town three days before my flight left. Everything was bigger than I thought. It was like what is said in Isaiah 55:8-9: "My thoughts are completely different from yours" says the Lord "and my ways are far beyond anything you could imagine for just as the heavens are higher than the earth, so are my ways higher than your ways and my thoughts higher than your thoughts."

My prayers were complex and desperate. I was still not entirely convinced I wasn't supposed to stay in Canada, or stay in America. I just wanted God to tell me which direction I needed to face so that I could head in that direction. I wanted to be where I would glorify Him the most and be able to grow and help others do the same. I asked for passion to burn in my veins, and grace to follow Him wherever He may lead me. I asked for an opportunity to leave behind everything to follow Him, even if it included me selling all of my belongings. I really wanted to be in God's will; I didn't want to be out of his step one centimeter.

In asking and praying, I found myself reading His word more and discovering more of His character and nature. I realized that this was what I need to be seeking; not how to control myself, but how to let God consume me. This doesn't discredit the importance of self-control, but it emphasizes the NEED for Christ, because on my own, I know I just won't have enough. In knowing more of Him, HE would be the one to make my character change.

I didn't need a list of do's and don'ts of how to live a merited life; those changes happen as we follow after Him. The Bible is not a list of moral codes, but a letter from the King of how to grow to know him more, and follow after Him. There are very practical applications that we can take to show how to conduct ourselves, but it is entirely important to KNOW the one who made it happen. This does NOT give permission to live however we feel, if we truly follow Him, He will direct our steps. It does not discredit the advice of Godly leaders, but shows us how to stand on our own and KNOW our relationship with our Savior. It is truly that personal, and truly possible to follow Him one on one.

The day before I left, I fasted. I spent the day going about as usual but I prayed and sought after the Lord more than I ever have before. I had to be sure this was correct. With the peace that God put over my heart, I knew I was going. I had to trust that God's plan would be accomplished in my journey. I wish I could have said I was unceasing in my prayers, but that would be deceitful. I did however spend more time and more specific focus on fervently praying.|

It seemed that God had organized another meeting with two

dear women that needed encouragement. I told them about the dreams that God had given about this trip and what was happening. I asked them to pray for the trip and their faith was also encouraged (at least this is what they have told me.) It is remarkable that one person's obedience also influences those around them.

I packed light (often packing and repacking); I took the smallest amount of clothes that I have ever taken on a trip. I didn't bring any jewelry other than my rings that I always wear and the eyebrow ring in my eyebrow. I didn't want to have to carry a large amount with me. I felt it important to travel lightly, besides the cost of a checked bag for a flight is out of this world now!

The next day was wonderful! Again, I must include a journal entry because I don't think there is a better way to share what God was doing inside of me.

My life is not my own, this trip is a continuation of Thailand. The dream happened there and is now coming true. It has been crazy all the thoughts going through my head today and I think I have settled into a weird state of being with the amount of fear that has hit me at the craziest times. I have to know it is Satan attempting to defeat me, because when I calm my mind and seek God, I am completely at peace.

Yesterday I fasted and felt so at peace. God has empowered me to be a blessing and find ways given by him to share on encouragement, even to teach on it, to build unity and help each other through the times. I can't forget this is to be an example of reckless obedience.

I have to get past this stupid fear of man. Who am I to fear humans when God is all knowing, all powerful? It is all about Jesus and I just need to follow Him. I know His purpose will be accomplished whether He uses me or not. I just so badly want to be doing what He wants!

I need to know and trust that the "why" doesn't matter; it is the being bold, being humble and willing, and following through on that willingness that does. God is so good! He loves his children and we are adored. He loves us too much to want us to live in complacency! Do what you are called to do, but LIVE! Do not tip toe! Dance, run, stomp, trudge, skip and frolic for the Lord for the Lord is above all our circumstances. (Shane Clairborne says it best in his book *Irresistible Revolution* "All around you, people will be tiptoeing through life, just to arrive at death safely. But dear children, do not tiptoe. Run, hop, skip, or dance, just don't tiptoe.")

SO HERE! In this airport, I have two more hours until boarding time. I love watching all the lives of these people, the kind of shoes they are wearing. Some are wearing shoes; no human should ever have to attempt to walk in let alone run a distance, in flip flops or running shoes. Some people are sad, and some people are so excited and seem to race toward something. This is it; this is all the life we have. This is a gift. So please, never settle for anything less than what the Lord Jesus wants.

All He asks for us to remove, he will not leave a void. He is good and His love wants to cultivate in that. It is true that we can never be good enough, but it doesn't stop there; we are COVERED in his grace if we chose believe, love, follow, and obey him. We get to love him, and we are given a chance to be used by Him to further the glory of his name and presence. How amazing is that?

Willing to Hear

At the airport I was continually reminded of a passage that was about being willing to hear. I looked up a few references for those words and came up with the following: Matthew 11:15 "Anyone who is willing to hear should listen and understand and if you are willing to accept what I say, he is Elijah, the one the prophets said would come." Matthew 13:9 (this passage is talking about spreading seeds) "Anyone who is willing to hear should listen and understand." The next reference is Matthew 13:43 (talking about mustard seed) "...then the Godly will shine like the sun in their fathers kingdom, anyone who is willing to hear should listen."

It stirred the inside of me when I remembered a message I got during church, not from the pastor, but from the Lord during the service. I wrote it down on whatever paper I could find because I knew it was important.

Let us not be vain or conceited and put our focus on things of this world! Even if we think it is for Christ! Let us move forward and be humble yet BOLD for the Lord! May we not limit the Lord Jesus to MONEY! He is triumphed over All! SHAME ON US! How dare we limit the Lord, how dare we gloat! It is not about our efforts; they are all just moments in the wind, a glimpse. Stupid humans, mere men, it is not about us, it is about God!

This message was not one of haste or hatred, but of love and a cry out of desperation and anguish that Christ has become so much about money; a profit not a prophet (he wasn't either, He was the Son of God, but I couldn't help myself with the word play.) God is so much more than anything! Jesus is the only one that is satisfying. He doesn't want us to settle, but instead, to wholeheartedly pursue Him, to go and make disciples of all nations, go as in action, as taking that step.

During the flight, the Holy Spirit was heavy upon my heart. I had three seats to spread myself over napping and listening to the most intense passionate worship music. I could feel his presence surrounding me, and my spirit was stirred. It wasn't about Canada. It was about going to the exact destination that God had worked out and established. He reminded me of the two dreams I had mentioned earlier; the one about encouragement, the airline code, the room with the guitar in the corner of the world and the second, a song.

He was reminding me of my confirmations and what was to come although he didn't tell me how it would come to pass. I thought back to Thailand when I asked God about Canada and the four people in the room burst into the song "Let's go to Canada." It was crucial that it did not become an idol, but a road map to help me focus on the task he sent me on. It is all about Jesus and relinquishing my rights, which is another conversation my friend and I had before I began the journey that he was speaking a lecture on. It was what God was also working on in my life.

I had to continually surrender the trip to God in case I had tried to take any of it back for myself. For the remainder of the flight on the plane, I prayed and listened to the worship music that my Mp3 player contained. I looked out my window and I heard the announcement that we would soon be landing. I was there. I was in Canada.

CHAPTER 16

Once my feet hit the ground and I made it through customs (at an extremely fast pace thanks to having only a carry-on), I began to see things that were very familiar such as the signs and the long corridors. These were not signs that are common to every airport; they are the ones that I had seen in my dream. My heart started beating faster. These familiar things were only familiar because I had witnessed them in a dream before I arrived! I knew I was in the right place and I knew my six days here would be an exciting and challenging time; I did not want to waste a single second of it.

As soon as I made it through the terminals, I found my friend Steve who was waiting to pick me up, along with his friend Anna, the leader of the school. I instantly liked her and was excited to see how she would fit into my time here in Canada. It was late and the drive back to the base was an hour long (during which I am certain I talked way too much; it was non-stop from Calgary all the way to a little town called Turner Valley, AB Canada). This was a quaint town with a few small restaurants, town shops, and a gas station. We passed the sleeping town and drove down a cute road to what used to be a hospital that had now been converted to a training school for Youth with a Mission (YWAM).

Stepping out of the car, I gazed to the sky. There were stars that I had never seen before. I got a quick tour of the base. As we went through the dark hallways, I couldn't see things quite clearly, but when they lead me down to the DTS (Discipleship Training School) classroom, my heart suddenly took a leap. Here it was. This was the room that was wider than long, had gray carpet, and a cross with a guitar standing in the corner. I knew that in the morning when the sun would shine through the window, it would cast a really cool light about it. Joy filled my heart! I knew this was the place that God had prepared me for, this occasion, and for whatever it would entail.

Then they lead me to my room for the week and it was a HUGE blessing. It had a large bed in it, a small table with chairs and a bathroom that would be all my own. This room was painted yellow, and even though it wasn't the exact color of my dream, I thought for sure this must be the place that I knew I would be lead to. I was overflowing with excitement, humility, honor, and many other emotions and I couldn't sleep. I fell to my knees and as quietly as I could, cried out to the Lord, thanking him for bringing me to this place. I was His to use as He wanted and asked him to show me what he had in store for me at the base. I suddenly felt the need to open my Bible and was drawn to these following passages, in this order:

Colossians 3:12-14 "Since god chose you to be the holy people whom he loves, you must clothe yourselves with tenderhearted mercy, kindness, humility, gentleness and patience. You must make allowances for each other's faults and forgive the person that offends you. Remember the Lord forgave you. YOU must forgive each other.

The most important piece of clothing you must wear is love. Love is what binds us together in perfect harmony."

Hebrews 10:24 "Think of ways to encourage one another to outbursts of love and good deeds"

Philippians 2:3-4 "Don't be selfish; don't live to make a good impression on others. Be humble thinking of others as better than yourself. Don't think only about your own affairs, but be interested in others too and what they are doing."

Philippians 2:5-6 "Your attitude should be the same as Christ Jesus had. Though He was God he did not cling to His rights as God."

Ephesians 4:2-3 "Be humble and gentle. Be patient with each other making allowance for each other's faults because of your love. Always keep yourself united in the Holy Spirit and bind yourselves together with peace.

I wasn't sure what these verses had to do with my time in Turner Valley, but I knew that they were significant. I wrote down the entire verses in my journal and held them close to my heart.

The next morning, I awoke and made my way to the DTS classroom to sit in on the weekly lecture. I was excited to see what this was all about. I had always desired to participate in a DTS of my own, and I was going to get a preview of what I would be experiencing. I had made up my mind to avoid the staff, because my heart was already tugging that this could have been task from the Lord to have been here. At this point I did not want any of them to know I had not only considered, but completely disregarded the strong urges to apply for this very segment of school.

I was already a week late into the class, the first week was about laying down rights, and relinquishing control to Christ and I did that at my house and life away from class in preparing for this very trip. It was remarkable to see how God was working on the same things while we distances apart. I had to lay down my ideas of what were normal and in the confines of my mind. God had been working in my heart the very same lessons that the other students were learning, only I was having private lessons with God. My struggles with coming, and my internal fights against coming were very much about laying down my thoughts and giving them over to God.

I came right in the middle of the week when they were learning all about hearing God's voice. I couldn't believe His timing; that He used my timidity to glorify Himself anyway. I came to Canada because I heard His voice; I was scared I was doing it wrong, but it still was used as an example of hearing what He had to say and following through with what was being told. It was another confirmation that I was in the right place, awkward, but cool.

The class period that I sat in on talked about the many ways that God communicates, uses his voice, and listens. He speaks to us in many forms to share his character. A great example of this can be seen in: 1 Kings 19 where the Lord is speaking to Elijah. I love that God told Elijah to go and stand before the Lord on the mountain because I was very close to the mountains and could actually get a sense of how this might be. The Lord sent a mighty wind; the rocks were blasted with a loud and terrible force, but the Lord was not in the wind. Then there was an earthquake, but the Lord was not in the earthquake, then a fire, and the Lord was not in a fire. Then Elijah heard God's voice; it was the gentle whisper that followed all of those things. God spoke to Elijah in a still, small voice.

I know often times we look to God for these monumental things that we know are him; I know I am fortunate that he spoke to me in my dreams. I have to assure you that it is very challenging to make sure that it is in fact the voice of God, and not my own heart. It takes much prayer and seeking to be sure that I have interpreted it correctly; a lot of pressure for sure!

I love all the ways that God communicates with us though! He speaks to us from His word, circumstances (sometimes), supernatural signs, visions, through creation and angels. He speaks to us in dreams, words of wisdom (which is when you or someone is talking and you JUST KNOW that it is God, not a boastful knowledge thing, and not to give you privy to others that could be used as gossip, but you just know) poetry, music, specific words of knowledge (where you can speak into someone else's life or when someone else knows something that they shouldn't in their own power) and impressions.

In all of the ways He speaks to us, talks with us, communicates with us, He does so directly to our minds with a great overwhelming peace. Despite the above listed ways that God reaches us, He isn't just limited to any of those things. He once had an arm appear out of thin air and write on a wall (see Daniel for this story. I wouldn't suggest asking God to send an arm to write on your wall, because that man in the story didn't survive for very long after…)

He certainly does speak to us in many forms, and on many occasions, but there are times when we don't always receive the message. There are many reasons why we don't hear his voice. Sometimes they are things that are caused by ourselves; our spirits get sleepy or become numb from whatever we have faced. So much so that it hardens us. Sometimes this comes from un-forgiveness, lie-based thinking, shame, tiredness, hopelessness and helplessness. I can't forget to mention drug and alcohol abuse or soul ties that go un-dealt with. In order to listen, to hear Him and His message, we have to rid ourselves of anything that offends the Lord, offer ourselves and acknowledge that he is always present.

I know it can get extremely frustrating not hearing His voice, or not being certain we are hearing it. There are many things that could cause this as well; we just have to trust in His timing and keep seeking Him. Sometimes we are asking the wrong questions like Steve in Thailand had done. He was asking about China, but God wanted to talk to him about the guitar. Like I do SO often in my life and God corrects me and answers something else. Sometimes we need to ask simpler questions (or just one at a time), and grow in trust, which also could mean that God has something more important to tell us first. Sometimes it means that we just don't need to know the answer. Someone else might need to be included in the process, which sometimes then involves factors that are related to others. Often, the delay is meant to teach something, but it is all to bring us closer to the heart of God.

Later that first day, we were given time to go and pray. I was going to head back to my room until Anna mentioned that there was a prayer shed down by the stream. Wait. What? Hold the phone a minute. There is a what? Where? Yes, it was true; this blessed base held the promise that the Lord would provide. My prayer shed was a place for me to pray before the Lord for as loud or as quietly, for as long or as short as I wanted. To this day, I miss that blessed little miracle, but I will get to that later.

I raced down the hill to find the lime-green yellow colored walls; the very color of the ones that were in my dream; wow. I fell to my face and began to pray; fervently thanking the Lord for bringing me here, as well as asking if he could please tell me what I should do with this week. I was no longer convinced that it was for only six days, but that God would complete his purpose for however long it would take. It had been less than 24 since I had arrived and already I had my prayer shed. In fact, everything I had hungered for was there, not in Wisconsin like I had previously thought the Lord would provide for me, but HERE in Turner Valley Canada (not to mention the body of water). All of my favorite things, the mountains, and a body of water surrounded by nature and now a prayer shack? I could hardly believe it all.

I prayed and shouted for joy, thanking the Lord for providing me with such a place. I knew that it wasn't the place I was so excited about, but the way that the Lord had used it to make me complete. I had stepped out in faith. He had heard my prayers and answered them to give me a place to pray. This is exactly what I had desired, a place to be alone with the Lord. I spoke to God through my heart and let Him take care of the words. His spirit and mine felt united and it was amazing.

I felt horrible for trying to negotiate with the maker of the universe that he had something up his sleeve; I have walked through fires and I get scared that I'll have to do it again. It seems that all the fires that I have had to walk through come to a stream of life and I am a little more refined because of it. I hate walking through the fire, and there will be another book about that. For the meantime however, I want to share with you the walk I had with God, how He chased me, pursued me and how I chased HIS heart. There have been many people in the Bible that have negotiated and God gave those people second chances; that is the only kind of negotiating that I want to do. I am not perfect in this; it's much like the verse that was the theme for this school: Philippians 3:12 "I don't mean to say that I have already achieved these things, or that I have already reached perfection! But I keep working toward that day when I will finally be all that Christ Jesus saved me for and wants me to be."

To tell you the truth, well more accurately, to keep telling the truth, I often get scared that I will hear wrong, act upon it incorrectly, or do something that would be offensive to the glory of God. I am so aware of his love and promise. There are often times when I just know it is him and then other times when I simply cannot believe it, or I am just not sure.

There have been too many occurrences in my life where everything that I have wanted and waited for, all of my desires and hopes somehow get sabotaged, so when something good does actually happen, I have to pinch myself to make sure that it is really happening. Or because I have found that my desire for that occurrence is so big that I get nervous that it doesn't line up with what God wants. I want to make sure that these things line up with each other and my desire doesn't get in front of what God wants to happen. I really am still striving, even while writing this, to continue to build my trust in the Lord. I know that when I fully trust Him, he can do all things. I would rather be in His way than any of my own.

While in the prayer shack, every time I tried to ask about why I was in Canada, I was not permitted to. It was like my soul put a stop on it, my mouth unable to put forth any sound or energy toward the subject. I couldn't pray in my head about it either. I was not supposed to be praying about that but was instead just supposed to be present in the moment to be patient and willing to seek out and let God reveal it in His own timing. The prayers that I was completely submersed in were seeking His heart, not the circumstances that surrounded it. My heart hungered and wanted to worship Him more and more. I kept feeling my heart being tugged towards the school application that I was going to fill out all those weeks before. My heart was also dealing with the fact that I was nervous to tell the staff.

In every class period that I attended, I observed the leaders. I knew that there were four female leaders and one male. What I did not know was that there was a guest speaker that I was counting on to be a staff member. I did everything I could to avoid them besides just saying hello. I wasted no time getting to know the other people in the building. I was in the hallway farthest from the DTS and spent my time there with the students that were in the School of Biblical Studies (SBS) getting to know them and just smiling at them. It was only my first day, but I knew that if I was there to bring unity, it was important to get to know everyone. Even if I didn't know HOW I would be bringing unity, I was doing what I could to act upon that prompting.

That evening was Wednesday night. Every Wednesday night was a time for Intercessory Prayer. Intercessory prayer is when you take time to listen to God and pray for others, locally, globally as you felt lead on the behalf of others. It was also a time to listen to what God would answer in response to the prayers. The DTS classroom was converted to a prayer facility, the only purpose being to come and sit in the presence of God. The focus was to pray for whatever God put on our hearts. I brought my journal and Bible in, sat down, and began to let my heart soften, releasing all my other thoughts so I could focus on Jesus. It reminded me of my time in Michigan when we went to the nursery at my church and just poured out our hearts.

Worship music was played and though others were in the room, it really was a time for unified, but individualized prayer. The manifest presence of God could be felt when we were all united in prayer, even if we didn't communicate them out loud; it was amazing! There was paper on the wall and table that we could also use to write down anything that God spoke to us. I didn't write anything at the time, but I was certainly perplexed by the negotiating I had tried to do earlier about waiting a year to do this DTS. I was certain I had missed my chance that this wasn't what God had wanted so I needed to be quiet the remainder of the week, and focus on the other things that God had brought me here for.

After I spent an hour in the room seeking God and praying, a girl came to my room with a piece of paper that she received in the room praying with a message that she felt God was giving to me. Since I thought I knew who all the members of staff were, I was encouraged to see a student come to me with this message. It was incredible; it held answers that I didn't know I needed. The note had my name on it as well as this message: "God is proud of you for following him here. Matthew 7:7-11. Keep searching for he has a good thing for you. It also had a drawing of a fork in the road, something old and something new, and a bible verse in Ezra that was about fasting. It was in those next several minutes after receiving this that my entire week would change, maybe even the course of my entire life.

CHAPTER 17

That night as I sat at my table, a student named Lory came in and sat down on the bed beside me. She handed me the note I previously mentioned in the last chapter. All of a sudden, my heart began to flame and I was suddenly at ease. I felt like at that moment, God told me to pour my entire heart out to her so as she sat on the foot of my bed facing me and smiling-that is exactly what I did. I told her I felt like I was supposed to be at the school and that I had disobeyed God in not applying.

I told her the discussions that I had with God about this school, how I wasn't even sure what I was doing there; I just followed God the best way I could. I told her that I couldn't possibly tell a staff member; what would they say if they found out that a stowaway had found her way to Canada, to the exact destination of a dream, and now had found herself in an extremely awkward position, not sure if she was supposed to stay or go.

In that next very moment, Lory smiled and laughed a little as she said, "Oh Diana, I AM staff."

I hid my face; I was embarrassed at the process of this all. She then proceeded to tell me that their prayers had been about the school. They had felt there were going to be nine students, and only eight showed up. Then all of a sudden, I show up at their school, the ninth student that they were praying for. My mind was spinning and I couldn't believe what had just happened. There was now a definite possibility that I would not be at this school just for a mere six days, but a whole school session. My heart was doing cartwheels as she left my room on her way to go find the other staff members to discuss what we had just talked about. She said she would inform the rest of the staff and they would pray about the things I had just told her.

If I were to stay, I would be starting the school over a week after the rest of the students and with no finances. Even though I would have to face these obstacles, I felt completely at peace about how God was going to work it out. He had already shown me the answer before I left.

That evening, I went in the SBS hallway and got to know a bunch of the students. It felt completely natural to get to know everyone. If I had only six days, I wanted to make the most of my time there and not miss an opportunity to get to know someone. I was doing my best not to reveal what had just happened in the meeting with Lory, but it was extremely difficult. I asked for prayer for direction from one of the students, and then we shared a bit of our life stories.

It was also the evening that I prayerfully decided that I would be fasting for 24 hours to really focus and commit to prayer. It was the most unique fast I have ever done in my life. My times of prayer were urgent, passionate, and my answers were always filled with "wait" of some sort. When the 24 hour period of time was over, my friend Christi and I broke my fast with a communion. We broke bread and remembered Him, but I had no wine or juice, so we used milk to remember His blood. It may be sacrilegious, but I can also tell you this communion was the most significant one in my life. It was one I was fully aware of all that God did for me, and it was between Jesus, Christi and me. It seemed that God was saying it didn't matter the elements that were contained in the communion, but the fellowship, repentance, remembrance and utter dependency on Christ.

Process

Sitting in the classroom, attending the classes that next day was an incredible thing; it was a whole new possibility. This was now a potential future instead of just a temporary arrangement. During that class period, we watched a powerful DVD about how indescribable God is. While I sat and watched, God spoke to my heart.

Again, I was not allowed to ask Him about staying. It was physically impossible but I asked Him if there was something He'd like me to share with myself and anyone else. My heart was elated with amazement of how big God really is, how big His love truly is, and how genuine His care is.

We are a mere speck of dust in a sunbeam in proportion to the extent of how large He is. What I felt Him saying was, "*Can't you see how much I love you? Can't you see My heart beats for you?! Oh please, Child, see how I love you! I want you. All of you. Can't you feel my heart or my tears? I want to give you my love, why won't you let me love you? Please, please allow me to love you to the fullest. I love you so much! Can't you see what you are worth to me? Can't you see that I moved Heaven and Earth for you? Please let me love you. Don't hide your heart, please let me love you. I've already made the way, but let me love you.*"

Cartwheels

I shared earlier in this chapter about cartwheels, and how they were jumping in my heart. I want to expand on that idea with you, to get your mind around what was happening and what God showed me through this experience. Before I had left for Canada, I had an experience with the cartwheel experience while I was talking to my spiritual brother in Christ.

We were talking about the Lord and how good He is; just lavishing in the Love of the Lord. My soul began doing cartwheels; not the giddy glee jump up and down feeling, but a literal spiritual cartwheel down to the depths of my being. I had gotten that same feeling the night Lory found out about the predicament of my staying, as well as whenever I read His word or hear a song about Him.

Bare with me. You might be saying, "Alright Diana, you are off your rocker; you are just a little excited", but this is so much more than excitement, more that I could ever attempt to fabricate. I know that I cannot make my spirit do cartwheels; I know this is from the Lord; it was a beautiful encounter with the joys he instills way inside of a person.

You might be wondering what my point is to all of this. Well, think for a second about a physical cartwheel. While you think about that, continue on with this before I go on.

That day while I sat outside, I wrote the following; a glimpse inside of my heart:

I am sitting at a stream and am at a bend in the river. It's still flowing; just the direction of the water has changed. Some of the gets trapped and takes longer to get around the corner and back to the regular flow. It's almost as if the water wanted to go to the right place, but it just got stuck.

I feel that I sometimes am this water; the whole stream that is moving is trying to get to Jesus, his heart, all of him and to follow him closely...

I don't want to be resilient, but I am not always sure where I am supposed to go. Sometimes I'll have moments where the rapids in my life are very exciting, but very rocky; I don't want parts to be buried or stuck behind something or miss a turn that I was supposed to make. Despite all of this, I know I bring God glory by letting Him love me. He made this stream He and made me. OH how he loves me.

It's not selfish to think this way. It's the very nature of the way God shows His love for us daily, as if we needed more than His son dying on the cross. God speaks to us in His creation, in the people around us, just everything. He created it all for our enjoyment and as a reminder to see him.

"Unless the Lord builds a house the work of the builder is useless. Unless the Lord protects a city, the guarding it with sentries will do no good.
It is useless for you to work so hard from early morning until late at night anxiously working for food to eat, for God gives rest to his loved ones...." (Psalm 127 the first few verses...)

Passion

This was where I was supposed to think about my passion; God has been stirring that in me for a long time. Here are a few things that I have vaguely written, wrote down and formulated Passion: Depth. A place for people to come rest in the Holy Spirit, be filled with him, and be sent anew...(this was where I heard in my heart. "Sounds a lot like YWAM" I literally laughed out loud) However, it's a little different because I'd like it also to be able to accommodate travelers, so they can have their own retreats and move forward. That, in addition to having a mobile part where we could travel and show God moving in other areas of the world to build more passion...

Do you think I have forgotten to tell you about the cartwheels? Well, you needed to read that before I could describe it fully. A cartwheel turns everything upside down, shakes things up and if landed correctly, can give you quite a pleasant thrill of accomplishment. God shakes our lives like a cartwheel at times.

Sometimes we need to get our feet off the ground and have our lives turned upside down. Sometimes we experience a perfect cartwheel where the flip goes well and we land on our feet. Sometimes we come down wrong and end up getting hurt. Even then, God allows us to learn, to grow from it, and execute it right the next time.

I have found that my feet often need to leave the ground so I can see more of what God would want me to see. I can get too focused in my little bit of pit I sometimes can get into, but in the times that God shakes us, he does it because he has something so much bigger planned. He shakes us so that we are able to gain some perspective and open our eyes to Him, his joy, and his truth, to just let it consume us. A cartwheel can change us, even if it is just a little bit.

Journals

I find it odd that my journals, without fail, come to an end of pages when a new chapter of my life is a new beginning. I will get back to this thought later in the story, but continue with saying I found it fascinating that my journal had only pages left when I arrived in Canada; I am glad that I had a new one along with me. I knew something would be changing; I just had no idea what it would look like. I only could pray and put it in the hands of the Lord as the staff sought him in what my place would be. I began the application process and made sure to do my part of what I might have to take care of if I were in fact supposed to stay.

I found myself outside by the stream again; sitting in the rocks, trying to figure out what God wanted me to do. I was surrounded by his creation. The foothills of the mountains reflected and shimmered in the stream; there were trees, and I felt like I was alone in the world with the maker. The beach was covered in detailed rocks that had been brought down the mountain over the last few decades. I suddenly became overcome with emotion that I no longer could stand. I did not want to be selfish. I wanted so much to be where God wanted me to be. I thought of what my life would be like if I stayed in Menomonie and completed my schooling, and I knew that it would be a great choice and I could glorify God there. I knew staying here in His wilderness could also accomplish the same.

I fell to my face on those rocks and asked God to show me which of the two choices he wanted me to do. My heart soon became at peace; I looked around again. I began to think possibly that this was the best place that God had brought me here for a purpose. There was something that He wanted to work on in me, use me for at the same time. Amazingly, my last entry of the journal was saying out loud that the choice I thought would bring God the most glory, would be staying. Even though, I still didn't know if that were the reality.

Leaving It All Behind

When I arrived home from Thailand, I felt overwhelmed with the amount of "stuff" that I had; it amazed me at how much I have in comparison to my friends on the other side of the world. All of these material things, this overwhelming amount of "stuff", it all becomes a burden when you have to carry it from place to place. I had asked the Lord for an opportunity to sell my belongings and follow him.

It appeared that this was going to be the chance to do that. I still had not been accepted into the school, and the staff kept letting me know what the next step was in the application process. I had a new challenge to face: trying to seek God and do what I could to make sure I was not missing my part of the task in becoming a student. If it turned I didn't get accepted to the school, I knew it was not because I hadn't forgotten to file a paper or an essay or something along those lines. I wanted to make sure that it was God that would do the work, and that I hadn't lacked in any task.

All the while as I was filling out the application, writing the essays, getting my transcript, and talking to my doctor (who was in a different country), I still felt that I had asked God about this event, and I was not to ask again. He had me focus on so many other things. I spent many hours in the prayer shed. I prayed for so many things, and without fail, every time I tried to bring up the topic of staying in Canada, I felt that I was not to pray about that. I struggle with having to prove myself, and God was showing me that He had to be completely in charge of this. There was nothing more that I could do at the time but trust Him.

I waited and continued interceding for others during my time in the prayer shed for three days. I was really enjoying my class time, and since I was still a visitor, while the others did their work duties, I spent the two hours in the shed praying. I was down on those rocks by the stream that I would go to so often and I was literally on my face and I found one small stone that had two perfect circles around it. I was looking at it and was intrigued by the design of this rock and was curious that God made it, this little rock.

It probably came from a larger one, but He was responsible for it being here at this exact moment. That was when I looked around again, and it hit me that I was surrounded by God's creation. This was a time that God had prepared for me to come, to sit aside and grow, to be used by Him; I had no idea how long it would go but it was wonderful. . I took a deep breath and really felt God surround me with peace.

That night, I read my bible, asking God if he would reveal anything that would stand out that he would like me to see. The verses that stood out to me in particular were from 2 Corinthians 1:17-22: "You may be asking why I changed my plan. Hadn't I made up my mind yet? Or am I like people of the world who say yes when they really mean no? As surely as God is true, I am not that sort of person. My yes means yes, because Jesus Christ, the Son of God never wavers between yes and no, He is the one whom Timothy, Silas and I preached to you and he is the divine –Yes- God's affirmation. For all of God's promises have been fulfilled in him that's why we say amen when we give glory to God through Christ, it is God who gives us along with you the ability to stand firm for Christ. He has commissioned us and has identified with us as his own by placing the Holy Spirit in our hearts as the first installment of everything he will give us."

I know context means everything, and this scripture spoke very loudly to me. I had thought that I had made up my mind, even if my heart hadn't been into it. I love that God gave me a second chance at this. God had used this to answer the question I had been persistent with. I had decided NOT to stay, that way MY decision, but God showed me HIS decision was different than mine.

Wembley

With the excitement of possibly being able to stay in Canada, I was also struggling between having my heart torn out; I would have to find arrangements for my beloved Wembley. My time with this pup had been so short, and I didn't think it was time to be without him. However, I would do what it took to be able to follow God. This became a challenge, and the most difficult thing about considering staying in Turner Valley. What would people think about me leaving my dog behind? He is my responsibility! I searched and looked for a home for Wembley, but God had different plans for this pup!

CHAPTER 18

Lord, it is coming to a close. This book, I feel it. I pray God that you would help me finish with great grace so that you get the most glory. I don't want to get any glory for this or have anyone get the wrong idea. I just want them to see your promise and what you can do when we follow you. Please let that be apparent in my writing. Please get the glory Lord, and let your kingdom grow because of this book.

God puts things in places at the right time. It was Friday evening and it was time to be "introduced" to Turner Valley. There was an exciting party that we had where we were to dress up in cowboy clothes and other awkward apparel that could be found in the closet located under the stairs, or at the consignment shop in town. I found a fun vest to wear and loved some of the other festive outfits that we came up with. It was really fun to be able to be a part of this welcoming night, even though I was still a visitor. The night was a great deal of amusement that didn't end when the party was over. A whole bunch of us spent some time in the cafeteria afterwards with a deck of Uno cards. We did not however, play Uno.

I was almost desperate to get to know these people that surrounded me and I feel that God gave me an idea to get to know them. In the process of this evening, I discovered things that had been hidden in my heart, that I had no idea where there, and the Lord used this game to bring them out. It is incredible to be able to share our hearts and lives and dreams with others. This also includes the many things that God has done. There is NO greater thing than talking about what the Lord does in our lives. There is no greater reward besides having Jesus in our lives period. It is about being able to share in the glory and in his goodness about what he does. He is the master of all things!

In that discussion over our Uno cards, I realized I had been afraid of doing DTS; I felt it was selfish to spend so much time devoted to a school when I wasn't even sure what the outcome would be. It felt that I was spending so much time on myself and my relationship with Christ, keeping it all to myself. I was so very wrong, and I didn't even know I held these things in my heart. It is not selfish to be able to devote time to getting to know the Lord. The more you know the Lord, and not just know *ABOUT* him, the more you want to share it and the more opportunities there are to give back to the kingdom. If I were to stay, it would be the first time in almost seven years that I wouldn't be a member of staff; it would be a completely different serving experience.

It also came up that God was preparing me for brokenness, a brokenness that strips away all of me and leaves room for him. I had no idea what this looked like, and I won't be getting into that in this part of the story. There will have to be a completely different book to discuss this process. Sometimes I try so hard to hold myself together when God tries to break me, to rebuild me. God was preparing a place for me to be broken, a place where I wouldn't try to hold myself together, a place where He could continue restoration in my life so God could bring Himself more glory. It was completely a challenge to be able to admit that I hadn't arrived just because I had followed Him this far. I had no idea what I was in for. I really did not feel that the school I had been going to would be the place to have these things takes place yet God kept holding my heart, stretching me more and more.

Desperation and deep desire kept my heart close to the Lord that evening as I went back to my room after getting closer to these new friends. I was sad at the shortness our friendship could really be, and I miss them as I write this, but I know that God is doing amazing things in their lives and I have truly been blessed to be part of that. I asked the Lord to prevent me from being selfish, let to His glory be present in order for Him to receive the most glory from my life.

I awoke the next day, after the morning session of class was over, and took a walk to explore my surroundings. I left with an Mp3 player and my camera. I couldn't get over the mountains that were close and the verses in the Bible that spoke about going up in the mountains to meet with God. I could really relate to the incredible experience of being surrounded by so much rock. It was an amazing connection of how much God is the rock, how un-movable it, and He, really is. Psalm 121: "… I lift my eyes up, up to the mountain, where does my help come from. My help comes from you, maker of heaven, and creator of the earth… I love it. I could see it, feel it, and taste it."

I walked and walked and walked. I walked in every direction for quite a while, and then I turned and walked back the other way. I found out later that I was just a few blocks short of discovering a different town when I turned around. I loved how simple and somber this little town was. At least for a season of my life, everything was basic and had such a homey feel to it. While I was walking, I was praying and seeking for direction and just listening, I began to reflect over how much had changed in the last four days. I had two days left of the original trip, and I began to feel a little unsettled. I wasn't sure if I had done everything that God had wanted me to do while there.

Rushing

I have to take a break from that thought for just a second and ask, "Do you journal?" If you do, you might be able to relate to this section a little bit more than if you don't. I will do my best to explain and describe it in a few different ways. Seeing as I talk about it all the time, I especially hope you can relate.

I know I mentioned earlier, but I feel it important to mention again that when I am in my journals and I am writing, I just let things happen with the words. I have a thought process and let it go. I write things down that I see and that I feel God teaching me. Something ironic that I have noticed is that whenever there is a major or simple life change in the chapters in my life, I conclude the current journal I am in. I don't attempt to do this, but it just seems to always happen. I have sixteen journals to date, sixteen journals that depict a lifetime of journey, one that has been incredible. I love looking back and seeing what God has done, what beautiful things I have been able to experience, and the terrible disasters that God has brought me through.

Even with that, when I get to the last few pages of the journal, I get an excited anxiety. My heart begins to rush and I can't help but wonder what is going to fill those last few pages. Sometimes I want so badly to fill those pages, to rush, because I know something else is up ahead. I'd like to think I could just 'write away' whatever unknown may be lurking in the distance. I know when I was in Canada, I tried to rush. I tried to close a chapter of my journal that wasn't quite ready; there was just a little more that God had to do with it. It is an exciting thrill.

As I write THIS part of the story, I know the time I spend with this title is coming to an end. I am excited and thrilled at the possibilities that God can do through this work of words. It has been a remarkable amount of time that I have poured into these pages, doing my best to retell the story of how God moved me and changed me and allowed me to follow Him. I am nothing more than a girl, or a woman, after God's heart that holds a pen in my hand, or in this instance, a computer on my lap.

I find myself getting that same excited feeling making me want to just keep typing until it is accomplished, but I can't rush. I can't rush the timing of God's work in this telling of the story. It is a beautiful thing that I love to witness. How even in this, God is working. There is still more to come! I don't want to rush through this segment of writing just because something else is coming along. I don't want to slack off in my writing just because the end nears. There is more to come. It's like a song, you can't have it too short or rush to finish it; it just won't come out right.

Sunday

Sunday was a very remarkable day. I was now within 24 hours away from my flight taking off. I went for a walk with a friend who became quite important in my mere five days of being in Canada. She and I shared a special bond that allowed us both to open up. It seems that God certainly did place us in this exact spot for this exact purpose. We prayed together and she shared with me that she really hoped that it was God's will that I stayed. I said I was willing to do whatever God wanted me to do and that it was out of my hands at that point in time. I told her I would be there in whatever way I could be, while still doing as God wanted. She thanked me for my encouragement.

That afternoon, I also had a meeting with my friend Steve

and the leader of the school. I used this time to really search my heart as they asked more questions about my life and why I felt God had wanted me to stay. I did my best to explain the same thoughts that I poured out to Lory. I didn't know if it meant that I was to be there for only six days or if it meant that I was to stay the remainder of the school year. I really, really, REALLY did not want to mess this up. I knew that my staying or going would not only impact my life, but the life of everyone on the base. It was just the same if anyone else was to stay or go. If I was to stay, it was going to have to be because God wanted it to happen, and not in an ethnocentric sort of way, but because if anyone else were to stay or go, it would also affect the dynamic of the group.

I spent a great deal of time in the prayer shed again that day, soaking up all that God would reveal to me. I meditated on the fact that we are children of His and His loving grace is so large. It took everything inside of me to not ask about staying or going, but just to soak in that moment. It was an intense and marvelous time of prayer and worship; I was certain my heart would burst if I felt any more of His grace and love around me. He held me with His promises in the Bible. It was phenomenal.

I took a walk down to the stream again and took it all in. That could possibly have been my last night in Turner Valley as I still did not have the answer if I was staying or going. I had to be prepared and just do what I could to make the most of my time.

That night was joyous for me. I invited everyone in the hallway that I was staying with to come over to my room. I love being a host and sharing my space, especially since the room I was given to live was HUGE. It was full of wonderful treats that I was so blessed to be able to share with the students in the hallway.

We laughed and laughed; it almost seemed like I had known these students all of my life. It was weird to think that it was possible

I would be leaving them the next evening. We played more games, getting to know deeper parts of each other and as the night dwindled, they prayed for me; that the events would come to pass just as God wanted. If I were to stay, let it be and if I were to go, let it be.

Shortly afterwards, a bunch of DTS students, as well as SBS students, went out to look at the stars. This particular girl named Sherry came out and we had the most blessed conversation that I had had over the course of my trip. We talked about life, the times that brought pain and also the times that brought joy. We also shared how much we had in common, how God had changed each of us because of a particular instance in our lives. There were two deer that came remarkably close to us while we were sitting out there. It was just so peaceful to sit out under the stars and soak in this moment. I absolutely loved this girl's heart, and was sad that we hadn't been able to spend more time with each other.

My heart jumped a beat as I saw Steve and Anna walking toward the larger building. I shouted a hello to them; I had a feeling they were coming to find me. There were a lot of things that needed to be done if I was going home, or if I was staying. It was now nineteen hours until my flight was scheduled to leave. They waved back and headed my way. They said that the staff had done much praying and had taken a break. I knew these words would soon change my life. I didn't know what to expect, I couldn't read their faces.

Then Anna opened her mouth to speak.

CHAPTER 19

I sat there, not sure which answer to expect or hope for. I knew that whatever was to come out of her mouth would be great; whichever direction God had me go in. It seemed like an eternity as my heart pumped blood through my body. The excitement of staying filled my soul; the anticipation of what that would entail jolted my heart. The thought of going home, knowing that God had accomplished all he shared with me in the dreams was thrilling as well.

I held my breath for a moment and she spoke. I still was in disbelief as I heard the words come from her mouth. She said that as a result of prayer, the staff felt it would a great thing if I were to stay and become part of the DTS class.

I let out my breath. Sherry leapt off the blanket and started jumping up and down and hugging me. I could NOT believe that this was the next five or six months of my life. A brand new reality was about to face me. I was not going home the next day. I now had a million new tasks that I had to face including being two weeks behind everyone else at school, as well as a host of so many other things.

I went back to my room at a fairly late hour, but sleeping would evade me. I would be moving in the morning, and my whole life would be turned upside down. I had to change my flight before I went to sleep. I asked when school would be over for the year so I could figure out my return ticket home. It cost a little money to change the flight to depart, this time six months from now on February 14. Another moment of reality; I no longer had a flight out the next day.

Sleeping that night in the guest room was interesting. I took the time that I couldn't sleep and packed my belongings, meager as they were. I was moving the next day to my new bedroom that I would be sharing, with someone else. I was still not sure who I would be sharing the room with, or how anything would work out. I had barely enough belongings for the six days I was going to be there as well as no winter jacket, but somehow I knew it was all going to be ok.

When I woke up in the morning, I was glad that I had already packed. I took my last shower in my room before I moved my belongings down the long zigg-zagging hallway to find the door that had my name located on it. I was overwhelmed with joy when I found that the girl whom I shared so much with last night would be my new roommate.

The next days were filled with finding arrangements for Wembley. I hated that this would be a burden for those left back in Menomonie. I even tried to find a permanent home for my beloved puppy. During my stay in Canada, he ended up spending half the time in two different houses. My friends will never know how much this meant to me and how God worked this together. I thank the boys of the "The Hidden Temple" house year 2008 as well as the girls of the "Pearl". Because of them, Wembley is sitting next to me right now as I write this. I won't go into detail in this part of the story, but I will say that I am so glad God gave me this dog and that he didn't have to go away forever.

I called the school administration board and found out the steps I needed to take in order to quit one school and become part of another because at that point in time, I was enrolled in two schools simultaneously. Dropping out of school was scary and intimidating, but I did receive a message from the woman in admissions with a huge amount of encouragement. She never would have been given the exciting opportunity to support someone if my email hadn't gone through her office. My signature on my email was Proverbs 3:5-6: "Trust in the Lord with all your heart and in all your ways acknowledge him and he will make your path straight."

This verse has become sort of a theme for my life. It seems that the more I trust Him the more He directs my path. Even if I don't really understand exactly why it looks the way it does. I keep it at the signature of all of my emails as a reminder to myself that God is in control, and hopefully an encouragement to all who receive an email from me.

I ended up putting everything I owned back in the states up for sale on the internet. I had been given an opportunity to literally sell my belongings and follow Christ in a completely different way. The following is a post from my blog; I feel it crucial that you can get a sense of everything that was going on in this transitioning season of my life.

This week has been a crazy, surreal week of God just moving in my heart and teaching me about His grace for Me. Oh, I know I need it! I know I need to function in it, and for the most part, I always thought I have but still, I haven't always taken the time to make sure I am receiving the grace before I try to go pour it back out.

THIS does NOT mean that I feel I am perfect; it is the opposite in fact, but my mindset has been slightly wrong in the way that I have gone about this. I have known, but that doesn't mean it is easy to accept the gift of grace in every single one of life's daily situations. This season is a time to spend completely invested in my relationship with the Lord, and He's showing me it's time. He's not doing it selfishly or as a burden, but instead, he has acted in way that has shattered all of the lies that I have been told and believed in, (thank the Lord.) He is bringing the truth to things that internally I have comprehended and applied to some extent.

So this is not making entire sense, but yet in some way it does. It felt selfish for me to set aside time and focus on my relationship when I have felt that there are so many people that don't even know Him a little bit! In the past, I have wanted so much for them to know Him that I have often sacrificed things that didn't need to be sacrificed but God is showing me that He does want to bless me and teach me! THIS season is for growth, for life, for US, me and Jesus. It's so weird, but wonderful, and I know that this will pour over into the rest of my life, on outreaches, and in making the gospel known. I have yet to spend more time with Jesus, but I am so glad that this is when and how God is doing it.

This week's topic in class was Identity, Destiny and Calling. Speaking of passions, I love that God was telling me things about these topics long before this week came. I feel sometimes I am resilient because I want to be sure it is God speaking and not just a fun idea someone got; I have been part of that far too many times and part of the opposite as well. I am realizing a lot of hurts that I have developed which make me more sensitive in a negative way, making me test everything far more than I need to. RELAX, D, it's ok! I feel like Jesus is telling me to just chill out and I will hear Him more and be certain it is HIM (isn't this fun that I get to be so insecure and vulnerable out here? But this is what is happening with the inner workings of me).

We were asked to think about our passions so I asked God what mine were. The first thing that He said to me was Depth. He then followed with a ministry that allows people to come along side of someone; a facility that allows for groups to come and rest in God, His Holy Spirit, in a nonthreatening way, and be trained, rested and restored, to go and share the Gospel, to multiply.

Also, this week, after the lovely personality tests that I normally dislike, I let my guard down and was blessed by them. I found that they were used by God to help reconfirm what He has given me for passion, purpose and a future. It was all spread out on a huge piece of paper which came down to show that my passions were:

Empowering others to Know God, and make Him known, missions...in a global sense, through counseling, teaching, music and leadership.

Stepping into a non-leadership/staff role has been interesting, but good. I am so excited for what God is doing in all of us here, the staff and students, and would love to know what is going on back home...

I have more things that God has been doing in the lives of everyone here; it's been amazing to see and be part of, especially because God is totally doing all of it. He's so good to us! It is completely foreign to take this time. It feels like a lot of time; to not have to be the staff, not have to be in charge of something, but instead just rest in the Lord and be trained. This time is RIGHT and GOOD, but it just feels so awkward (as I knew it would). Please pray for me to stop fighting it because I really don't want to! I know it's good!

FREEDOM

Where the spirit of the Lord is, there is freedom.

This freedom is from self, condemnation, and sins that have been committed against you. It is freedom from lies Satan speaks, insecurity, pride, gluttony, abuse, and freedom from the past, freedom. Freedom! Freedom! Freedom! Freedom!

That week had been amazing. It had also been one of the most challenging weeks ever of my life. I am still working through this revelation that God wants not only to work THROUGH me, but IN me as well, because I am a member of His kingdom, a chosen vessel, a DAUGHTER of the Highest...

Let me tell you about some of the process of this revelation. God is far bigger than all of this and again, I hope the Holy Spirit bridges gaps and that only He can receive glory for the work He is doing.

At the beginning of this week, we were asked a few word associations, the first word being “friend”. I came up with a lot of words that related to “friend” but for the second word, “father”, one word in particular, the first word that came to my mind, was "gone". Even though several other words came to mind right after, I immediately knew then that this was going to be a week that God was going to work in ways beyond my comprehension. I started crying at the realization that I still somehow held God in that view. I didn’t do this on purpose; I know that He is always there, but internally, there was definite a lot of hurt stemming from my relationship with my dad. I tried so hard to not let it bother me, but it was just that word. TRY. Jesus has to do it.

My father did an amazing job with what he had to be my father. My dad is an over-the-road truck driver that had to be gone way too much for both of our likings. I wish with all my heart he could get off the road and pursue the dreams that consume his heart. I love my dad and God has definitely continued working miracles in our relationship since then. Please don't hear this wrong, my dad is a fantastic father and I know that I am loved, and I love him. I am just trying to speak the realities of having a working dad that means having to spend a great deal of time away from his children.

On Tuesday night, during our evening lecture, Jesus spoke to me again and brought me to a place of brokenness and realization. We had time after class to just sit with music playing, to just sit still with God. He poured out His blessings and let me see the hurts in my life the way that He has allowed me to feel strong when I haven't been. He showed me that by being strong for everyone else, and for always taking care of others to the point where I was no longer taking care of myself that I had NO IDEA what it looked like to be a daughter of a King. . . That's huge and a welcome revelation... Wow. This was a fierce blast of emotions and reality . . . and more tears.

I love that tears are so humbling and healing, as well as all of the other stuff they bring. I also love the way God brings things up at just His right timing. At every point in our walk of faith, it seems He always seems to surprise us with what needs to be dealt with next. Sometimes these are things that sound like common knowledge and we feel like we should have a grasp on the concept, but God brings us to a deeper place with Him as we go through these discoveries.

The next night was even more intense; it was a night of confession, repentance, forgiveness . . . and FREEDOM.

I won't go into the details of this night but it was great. I could try to put into words the intensity that I was feeling, the good things that were occurring, but I don't know the right ones to use; just know that God was doing a work of healing on that base. He healed the wounds of His children and that have limited what both they, and myself, were able to do. It has been beautiful....

I did have a realization though that I can share; I know that God is above all things and so much bigger than anything I can even put into words, yet I still cannot grasp that even a little bit. As I ponder my thoughts on my father, and God as the father, somehow I have limited Him in that. My dad has been and is still a provider; he has sacrificed time, memories, and our childhood. I know it was because he was doing what he thought he had to do but internally, without realizing it, I have associated God with that same kind of system.

I KNOW inside that God won't have to sacrifice time spent or in any area in order to provide, but still my heart was/is cautious. This is something I am still working out with prayer; feel free to join me. God as a father has been so much of an opening awareness as opposed to God as a master or God as a friend. God as a father has allowed me to discover a brand new kind of love and it has been beautiful. I have always thought of God as a father, but didn't really put it together that it meant that I was a DAUGHTER to HIM.

I love that God is so relentless. It is so awkward sometimes thinking that I have somehow not gotten all of this in its entirety in all my years of teaching and helping. I love that God is never finished working in us as He works through us. I love that He loves us so much, and I just want the world to know, God's nation, the whole world. I now could see HOW important it was for me to be there right at that time. I know that God has used time to enable me to go and empower others in Him.

HE is so much bigger, bigger, bigger, bigger, bigger, bigger, than we can ever even imagine.

That's my Jesus.

CHAPTER 20

Though I would love to tell you every single thing that happened in Canada, I know that this part of the story ends here. I think I gave you an adequate summary that will allow you to get an idea of some of the things that can happen when you follow the Lord. He does amazing things and our lives can be the product of following Him. Canada was not an easy time for me, but it was good. God did so much, establishing many relationships that I will forever treasure, most of which I still am in contact with and I wouldn't have it any other way.

Living in a foreign country, with six days worth of belongings, not knowing what comes next, and just doing the best you can with what you have in front of you is a freeing experience. I was not tied down by all of these worldly possessions that I have had. It was also a challenge as well; I missed some of the comforts that I had gotten used to back home. I had no blankets that were my own. I had blankets and they were wonderful, but they weren't mine, the ones that I loved and were used to. It was a humbling experience and I don't think I would have grown as much if I had been able to prepare for the Canada trip like this.

God took my disobedience and turned it into something beautiful when I repented. He did this both in Thailand at the beginning of this story, and in preparation for Canada. Overcoming the fear that lead to my blatant disobedience is still something I struggle with. I know in each of the stories I mentioned earlier, if I would have been able to overcome the fear, the outcome would have been different. I know for instance, it would have been a messy process if I applied for the school in Canada the exact moment I was feeling the strong urge to so. God showed me twice how He still accomplished His purpose; He had me in Canada for exactly the amount of time he wanted me to be there. There were many challenges that came with being there, such as raising financial support to pay for the lecture phase and outreach portion of this school. Praise God for His faithfulness that gave me the courage to trust and how He overcame all my fears.

On November 10, 2008, I talked to my grandmother for the very last time. I was so happy to hear from her and at that time, I did not know that it would be the last chance I would have to talk to her. My grandma had many cancers that had spread through her body, plus a plethora of other health issues. I won't touch on too much about the loss and grief that came from my grandmother's passing for this comes in the next part of the story which is not contained in these pages. This was also the day that God asked me if I was willing to give up my outreach portion of the school. I did not know that would actually be required of me.

On November 17, 2008 I got the call from my mom that my grandmother was gone. My grief was large and painful. I was not able to fly back to Wisconsin for her funeral. If ever there was a time of being given the opportunity to follow Jesus, this was that chance for me. I wanted to go back with everything that was inside of my being. It was HARD, painful, and I still am not fully sure that I understand the reasoning in why I was not able to get home. I do know that God allowed me to be a part of saying goodbye from over a thousand miles away, and that God was glorified in my absence. In my emotions of knowing I wouldn't be able to go to her funeral, I sat at the computer and let my fingers pour out a message about my grandmother. When the reality of not being able to go set in, I revamped the words of my message a little so that it could become one to share at her funeral. Even though the pastor did not know what I had written about, my message was a bridge to what he had preached. Of course, this was an act that God completely orchestrated to show me His love and glory but it was still a personal heartache. Three days after she passed away, I received an envelope from her with a napkin and some money inside of it. I have never thrown that envelope or napkin away because it still reminds me of her, and what God did through this.

I began to prepare for the outreach portion of DTS, even though God had asked if I was willing to give it up. This outreach program would have been an opportunity to bless someone else. I had thought maybe it would be like an Abraham/Isaac experience (see Genesis for more details): God brought Isaac to the altar and put him on it. All at once, God stopped him, and there was the provision of the sacrifice. In my situation, I thought I would be completely willing and ready to give it up, and think that I had given it up, but maybe at the last moment, God would provide the means to continue. This was not to happen however because God had other plans. He had me return to the states as part of a different outreach portion and serve and help my mom who had been in a car accident. I was short just a little money for the trip, but I had enough to stay for the amount of days that God had me there. God fulfilled his purpose. It was hard to accept that a promised amount of money didn't come in, but God still worked it out for His purpose.

This entire story was the beginning to my life being taken and shaken.

The very last day that I was in Canada with the class before returning for what I considered my outreach portion of the trip, we had prayer time to send off the teams that were going to their destinations. The base had a time of prayer where they prayed for me as well. I can say that this was the most amazing confirmation; that I had come and done what the Lord had wanted, no matter how difficult it had been. Remember, I had not told anyone the reasons why I had come to the base, not the deep meanings (to refresh your memory, it was to teach on encouragement, bring unity, and be an example of reckless obedience.)

During the prayer time as they were sending me off, my heart was breaking. I wanted to go to Thailand again with the team that would be going without me. Once they started praying for me, tears began to fall and I joined them in prayer. Two people, including the director of the entire base, thanked God for using me to teach about encouragement. We also had a class period earlier which featured the 'Wall of Fame'. The 'Wall of Fame' allowed everyone a chance to get to say in which way they were able to impact the class positively. This was an amazingly humbling experience because it was here where they told me I had unified the group. God used me as the bridge which made the group a whole; before it was just two parts with something missing. I cannot tell you how much this humbled my heart. God had used me and had accomplished the things he had said would come, even though it didn't look the way I thought it should.

The final kicker of God's amazing grace was when Steve was praying for me; I will never forget his words. They were words that I know for sure came directly from the mouth of God; no one else would have known to confirm them and it is because of them, that I will forever be changed… "Thank you God for using my sister as an example of reckless obedience."

www.ingramcontent.com/pod-product-compliance
Ingram Content Group UK Ltd.
Pitfield, Milton Keynes, MK11 3LW, UK
UKHW020129250726
13967UKWH00002B/561

9 781257 062287